Broken but Made Whole

Cheryl Ann

Master's Publishing Company

Broken but Made Whole
© 2014 by Cheryl Ann

Published by Master's Publishing Company
Bethel Park, Pennsylvania

Library of Congress Control Number: 2014943763

ISBN: 978-1-940243-46-7

All rights reserved. No part of this book may be reproduced or transmitted in any form or by any means, electronic or mechanical, including photocopying and recording, or by any information storage and retrieval system, without permission in writing from the author.

Scripture taken from THE HOLY BIBLE, NEW INTERNATIONAL VERSION ®. Copyright © 1973, 1978, 1984 by International Bible Society. Used by permission of Zondervan. All rights reserved.

Holy Bible, New International Version®, NIV® Copyright © 1973, 1978, 1984, 2011 by Biblica, Inc.® Used by permission. All rights reserved worldwide.

Dedication

This book is dedicated to God the Father, God the Son (Jesus), and God the Holy Spirit, who gave us the strength and opportunity to write this book and bring us to victory. God, most importantly, you taught us to trust in you, walk in faith, believe in you, and stand on your holy Word and promises. All glory and honor is yours, Almighty Father. We thank you and love you in the precious name of Jesus.

I also dedicate this book to my daughter, Stacie. You never gave up when you faced adversity. You spoke to your mountains and trusted God, and through it all, you gave God the glory and He gave you the victory. I love you with all my heart and remember that you are very special. Stacie, I am truly blessed to have you as my daughter.

I also dedicate this book to my daughter, Nicole. You stuck beside us always, in every bad situation we faced. The joy of the Lord was your strength to keep us motivated and strong. You never gave up on Stacie and I, and were always there for us. I love you with all my heart and always remember how very special you are. Nicole, I am truly blessed to have you as my daughter.

I also want to dedicate this book to Pastor Spence and Julie. Pastor Spence, you dedicated your life to the Lord, and your youth ministry. Through your compassion, strength, caring, and love you have shown us, we were able to get through the trials we faced. You have an incredible way of teaching how to live, walk by faith, and stand on God's Word. We were able to persevere as God spoke through you. Julie, you were always there beside Pastor Spence, encouraging us also. The love from both of you to Stacie, Nicole, and I, is very special and we are very thankful for both of you. We love you. Thanks for letting Stacie be your adopted daughter.

Table of Contents

Preface vii

Introduction. ix

Chapters. 1

   1. Journey of 10,000 Steps 1

   2. Feeble Cry (Ann's View of That Day) 9

   3. Miraculous Birth 13

   4. Unexpected and Unknown. 15

   5. Battle Won 21

   6. Light of the World 23

   7. Early Stages of Ann. 25

   8. Fight for Ann's Life 29

   9. Another Mountain to Climb. 35

   10. Looking for Answers 41

   11. Missing Piece of Life Found 43

   12. Complications Set In 47

   13. A Tug at My Heart. 49

   14. When the Doctor Gives Up. 53

15. Another 1,000 Steps.............................. 57
16. Gift of Life.. 59
17. Decision of Doctors............................. 63
18. God Working Behind the Scene 65
19. A Distance I Could Not Reach on My Own 69
20. Struggles of the Journey 73
21. Keeping the Faith............................... 77
22. Why? (Ann's View of That Day) 83
23. Trusting God's Hands........................... 87
24. Listening from the Heart 89
25. Not Sure (Ann's Thoughts Before Surgery)....... 93
26. God Works in Mysterious Ways (Ann's Words) ... 95
27. Miracle of Miracles 99
28. When the World Says No, God Says YES 105
29. The Grace of God 107
30. God's Truth Is Marching On (Ann's Words)...... 111
31. Miraculous Life of Ann Continues............... 113
32. Laughing in the Devil's Face 119
33. He's Better than a Doctor, He's Our
    Marvelous God 121

Preface

This is a miraculous story of Ann and the glory of God. Ann has the spirit of a finisher. Anyone can begin a journey, but champions of faith finish them. Ann has always had the determination to go the distance, regardless of the obstacles she faces to finish with God what He has called her to do: become a youth pastor.

Ann, Elizabeth and I learned to face problems together. We have found out that the trials and difficulties of life turn into tomorrow's blessings. What the devil has meant for harm, God has turned around for the good. We have found our strength in God, and each other. We learned that no matter what the doctors say, God always has the last word. The determination of faith in God's Word and His promises is what has kept our family victorious. God is not finished with Ann's life and she will be the champion God wants her to be. As you read this book, I pray that you will be blessed and your own heart gripped to be the champion God wants you to be.

Introduction

I walked into the waiting room and just stood there. As I looked at Belle, fear came over me. I knew this was going to be a long ten hours, but at the look of relief on Belle's face, I knew Ann was going to make it out okay.

I sat down and reached for my Bible to read a verse that would soothe me. As I did, it felt like hours had passed, but it had been only minutes. Belle said, "Let's get your mind off this and go grab some coffee in the cafeteria." I knew that I needed to clear my mind but for me, the place to be was in the waiting room. Belle understood and went to grab us coffee.

While she was gone, I asked the nurse for a progress report on Ann's surgery. The nurse proceeded to tell me that Ann's blood pressure had dropped and there were complications. Surgery would take a little longer than expected.

I headed back towards the waiting room. As I sat down, I knew that the doctors could not heal Ann...only God could.

1
Journey of 10,000 Steps

What a beautiful morning! The sun is shining, and it's nice and hot. I love this weather. I have another cup of coffee and then get ready for work. Half an hour later I'm ready for work, my coffee to go is ready. Oops! I almost forgot to say goodbye to the girls. "See ya' later!" I say, even though they are asleep. "Girls, I'm leaving for work. See ya' later! I love ya'! I'll call you on my break." I wonder if the girls even heard me. I hope so. Today is Friday and the girls and I have to do something fun tonight. I'll have to think of something fun to do and suggest it to them to see if they are interested.

As I drive to work, traffic is horrendous. For a Friday morning there sure is a lot of traffic. I hope I'll be on time. I finally arrive at work...on time. "Praise God," I say out loud. I say hello to everyone, get another coffee, and sit down at my desk. My boss comes over and tells me, "I need you to enter these reports into the computer, and have it done by lunch. Don't forget to call these clients also," she said handing me a 5 page list of names and numbers. I have a lot of work ahead of me, but it's Friday and I have the weekend off with the girls. I am happy.

It is now nine thirty a.m. and my boss comes over to our department to tell us there is too much work to finish by day's end and offers overtime to anyone who wants to work over the weekend. Cindy are you going to take advantage of the overtime, I would but I have worked every weekend for the past two months and I am spending this weekend with my girls.

I follow my daily routine. Our phones ring off the hook. Reports need completion. Clients need to be called. Ugh! It never stops! Finally, it is break time. I go outside with my friends and call the girls. They are not awake yet. In no time, break time is over. (Fifteen minutes is very short when you are on break.)

Back to work I go. The next time I look up at the clock, it is Noon. Just then, the phone rings. It is Dr. Luke, my daughter Ann's neurosurgeon.

"Cindy—I need to speak to you in regard to Ann."

"What's wrong?"

"Cindy, Ann's tumor has grown rapidly. You have until 8 a.m., Monday to make a decision."

"What?" I exclaim, in alarm.

"You have until 8 a.m., Monday, to make a decision regarding Ann. You can either watch her die or let us perform an operation to save her life. Let me finish before you say anything, please. You need to know the risks of the operation: There is a 1 percent chance she will die on the table, a 1 percent chance the tumor will hemorrhage, a 15 percent chance she will suffer paralysis, a 25 percent chance she will experience personality change, a 50 percent chance her eyesight will remain the same or get better, and a 90 percent chance her headaches will go away. I will have to cut out the new tumor growth which has branched out into her cerebellum on both sides of the brain, being very careful not to damage the parts of the cerebellum the tumor has attacked. I will leave the part of her tumor in her brainstem because no one can touch the brainstem—that part of the tumor is inoperable.

"How can you call and tell me this?" I ask, in total shock.

"You always told me to be honest with you, and I am."

"But this is Ann we are talking about. How can I make a decision like this? I am a single mom! How do I know what to do? This is too hard for me to hear—that my daughter is dying sooner than expected. All the while I've been, taking her to doctors, helping her and encouraging her. This is a devastating call!" After a long pause, I continued, "Dr. Luke, I have to talk to Ann. We have no family. This is going to be a very hard decision—one I never thought I would have to make. How do you expect me to make the right decision?"

"Cindy, her tumor has grown to the size of a tennis ball and there is new tumor growth. You have to act fast. You have no time to waste. I know this is hard for you, but I know you will make the right decision. I've told you everything I know. I plan to hear from you Monday, 8 a.m. sharp, with your decision."

"I will call you then," I said, hanging up the phone. I am devastated and just stare into space as tears roll down my face.

I tell my boss that I have to leave, that I have an emergency at home and leave my desk with all the work still on it. I cannot speak to anyone. I run down the steps, no time to wait for the elevator, and run to the car. All I can think about is getting home to Ann. The world does not matter to me. The only thing that matters is getting home immediately. Over and over, I say to myself, *Why? How? What do I do? Why has Ann's tumor grown so rapidly? Why were doctors unaware of this before now when she has seen doctors constantly?* Hysterical as ever, I cried out to God, "What am I supposed to do?"

Thank God for cell phones. As I drive, I call one of the pastors of our church and explain to him what Dr. Luke told me.

"You have to give this to God," he advises.

"But this can't be happening!"

"Cindy, you are a very strong person. I will pray that you make the right decision."

This does not calm me down. All I know is that I have to get to Ann. Even driving like a maniac, I hit every red light. *Can this day get any worse?* I finally get home and run into the house, screaming for Ann. She comes running.

"Mom, what's the matter?"

"Ann, we need to talk, now." She could tell I had been crying and that something was terribly wrong. "Where is Elizabeth?"

"She's upstairs watching TV."

I screamed up the stairs, "Elizabeth, when we get back we need to talk! We will be right back, so don't go anywhere."

Ann hadn't eaten dinner, so I took her out for food at a drive through. Then we went to sit in the parking lot of a local shopping plaza to eat. Ann begins to eat, then stops and asks me what is wrong. I begin to cry and tell her we need to talk.

"What, am I dying today?" she asks.

"Ann, Dr. Luke called me today. We have until 8 a.m., Monday morning to make a decision. Your tumor has grown. He said that you must either have the operation or you will die." I explained everything to her that Dr. Luke told me. She begins to cry.

"It is so hard for me to make this decision," I tell her. "Of course I am not going to let you die, but how do I know—how do we know the right decision? I keep replaying in my mind the phone conversation between Dr. Luke and I. I try talking to God, but I can't hear what He is saying."

Ann asks me again, "What are the chances I will die?"

"One percent," I answered.

"Let's go for it!"

"But, you don't understand all the risks!"

"Mom, you always told me that you would do anything to save my life," she said. This pierced me.

How could I let her down? I think to myself.

We drive home and I tell Elizabeth what is going on. She gets extremely upset.

"What are you going to do?" she asks.

"I am still trying to figure everything out." As I say this, in the back of my mind I think that the operation is the way to go, but the consequences of it bother me a great deal.

"Mom, do what you have to do. We will get through this"

"Elizabeth, what if I make the wrong decision?"

"Mom, you won't. I'll be here for you."

At this, I give her a big hug and say, "Thank you! We will do what we have to do."

The risks of the operation weigh heavily on my mind, especially the one regarding the personality change, and the risk of becoming mean. Ann has always been a very happy little girl, always smiling, not a care in the world, and full of life. She is always singing, caring, and never mean. How can I let her have the operation if it causes her to become mean? What am I going to do? I am surely not going to let her die, but I refuse to do anything that will cause her to become mean. Though there are other possible risks of the operation, the personality change is not letting me go. I think to myself, *This is extremely serious. I have to make the right decision.* The three of us, Ann, Elizabeth and I, discuss this all Friday night.

It is now late Friday night. I am crying out to God. "How can you let this happen to Ann? If we have the operation, she will become mean. God, you know Ann has always been happy, never ever mean, always caring, and full of life. Please don't let her become mean. If I don't allow the operation, she will die. God, why was there no warning—no nothing? Why? Don't let this happen!" Suddenly, I hear God's voice and can honestly say He is mad at me. In a very strong, stern, loud voice He says, "I AM THE POTTER!" His voice is loud (I mean, LOUD). *I'm in trouble...God's mad*, I think to myself. *He speaks again*, "I AM THE POTTER! READ THE BIBLE." I am so afraid because I know I hurt God by looking at the circumstance and listening to the world, and not Him.

Minutes later, I start looking for my Bible. I always sleep with my Bible, it's like my security blanket, but I do not have it with me tonight. I look and see it on my nightstand. I abruptly get out of bed, pick it up and look up "potter," finding Isaiah 45:9-12.

> Woe to those who quarrel with their Maker,
>   those who are nothing but potsherds
>   among the potsherds on the ground.
> Does the clay say to the potter, "What are
>   you making?"
> Does your work say, "The potter has no
>   hands"?
> [10] Woe to the one who says to a father,
>   "What have you begotten?" or to a mother,
>   "What have you brought to birth?"
> [11] "This is what the Lord says— the Holy
>   One of Israel, and its Maker: Concerning
>   things to come, do you question me about
>   my children, or give me orders about the
>   work of my hands?
> [12] It is I who made the earth and created
>   mankind on it.
> My own hands stretched out the heavens;
>   I marshaled their starry hosts." (Isaiah
>   45:9-12, NIV)

I immediately break into tears, repenting and apologizing to God. I ask Him to forgive me for believing the doctor's words over His words. I talk to God, expressing how I felt and He gives me peace.

2

Feeble Cry (Ann's View of That Day)

I remember the day like it was yesterday. Mom picked me up from the house and said we needed to go get something to eat since I hadn't eaten dinner, and that we needed to talk. I was not feeling well. I could tell mom had been crying. Mom took me to get something to eat. We went to the drive through, got our food, and drove to the grocery store parking lot. I just knew something was wrong. We parked the car and mom began to cry.

"What's wrong? Am I dying today?" I asked.

"There's a possibility of surgery."

"What's the surgery?"

"Resection of half the tumor."

"What's the chance I'm going to die?"

"One percent."

"Let's do it. You said you would do anything to save my life."

"But Ann, you don't understand all the risks." She then proceeded to tell me all the risks.

"There is a risk of paralysis, personality change, cognitive delay, coma...even death." We discussed only the death part.

"Mom, I don't want to die. I know normally we would pray about it, but there isn't enough time." Mom rambled on about what Dr. Luke said the surgery would do, but I interrupted her. "I am all for it, Mom. God is a lot bigger than the risks. I am trusting Him to save my life. Mom, you said that you would do anything to save my life."

"Yes, but I am not losing my happy Ann."

"You won't. It's only a 25 percent chance. God won't let it happen."

"So you want to go through with it?"

"Yes, I do. Nothing is going to happen."

Well, at least I hoped nothing would happen. *My personality can't change—God wouldn't let it. I can't become paralyzed. How would I get to my room? I'm not going to die. Maybe I should talk to God now, this is scaring me so much. Dr. Luke said he couldn't do surgery and now he can. It doesn't make sense. He already said all possible surgeries wouldn't work. The tumor is inoperable. I don't understand how he just, like, invented a surgery and is going to try it out on me. I know Pastor Georgia gave me the verse, (Psalm 118:17 NIV), "I will not die but live, and will proclaim what the Lord has done." I will stand on this verse, but I am scared. What if God does take me home? I don't want to leave my mom. Last week, I was told I have six months to live, and now I have the weekend? I don't understand what you are doing God—I don't understand at all. Why do you want me dead so badly?* I didn't understand it at all.

Why had mom told me this right when I was about to eat? Forget eating. I was sick to my stomach and feared I would throw up.

"Are we going to meet with Dr. Luke before the surgery so we can talk this over?" I asked.

"Yes, on Monday. He will perform the surgery on Tuesday if I call him back and say yes."

I promise you, my life flashed before my eyes. You know how people say that just before they were in a crash or bad accident their life flashed before their eyes? Well, that happened to me right then.

Mom drove us home.

Then I told God something I had promised I would never say to Him: I told Him what I was never going to do. I told God I wasn't going to do anything with my life, and now that I only had until Monday, I was never going to graduate high school—I wasn't even going to graduate middle school. If I did survive surgery, I feared I would never be able to walk again. If I couldn't walk, I wouldn't be able to drive, get a job, dance—nothing. I thought I would never get a real boyfriend, get married, have kids—none of this. I would rather die than be paralyzed. I thought there was no way I could live like that. I feared I would lose all my friends. One of my friends, Landon, has been in a wheelchair for a long time. Maybe it won't be as bad as I am thinking it will be. On second thought...it will be bad. I won't be able to do anything.

We finally arrived home. I didn't want to deal with any of it right then. Perhaps if I pretended it was not happening, things would be different, right? Ugh! Maybe if I went to a friend's house I would forget about all of it. I assumed Sutton and Monica were busy and decided to go to my friend Natalie's house.

After about an hour, I walked home. I felt a little bit better because her family said they would pray for me, yet I was still unsteady about it all. I had told Natalie I didn't want to go through it. She then told her mom and dad, but I didn't mind. They asked when the surgery was, and I told them. I said I would call them after my surgery or the day after. *It's a ten-hour surgery. I'll call them the day after it. That will be better,* I thought.

I knew God would be there with my mom during my surgery, but she needed a person there, too. Elizabeth doesn't like hospitals (never did). I do not want mom to be in this by herself.

Maybe this is all a bad nightmare, I will wake up in the morning and it will be all over, I thought. Ha ha! I could only wish.

3

Miraculous Birth

Every day creates history. This, my friend, is the miraculous story of Ann and the glory of God.

Who is this Ann? Is she dead? Is she alive? Where is she? (Are you ready for suspense, drama, excitement, and happiness?)

Let's start at the very beginning and turn the clock back twenty-four years. I was so very happy to find out I was going to be a mom again. Though we had two children, a boy and a girl, I had miscarried four babies. After my fourth miscarriage my doctor had told me, "Cindy, you cannot keep having babies, the pregnancies and miscarriages are taking too great a toll on your body."

"You don't understand," I said. "I am happiest when I am pregnant. I know the love I feel with each child. I know the babies can feel my love. It's a comfort for me."

"We both know you have a bad marriage, but babies aren't the answer. I'm worried about your health," the doctor replied.

God brought me love through my children and that is why He gets the glory. No one understood that the only time I felt loved during my marriage was when I was pregnant, or holding a child close to me.

About a year later, I got pregnant with Ann. I went to the doctor to confirm my pregnancy and it was positive—yes! I was incredibly happy, though the doctor warned me this would be my last one.

A couple of days later I started to bleed. I called the doctor and went in for a sonogram immediately. He informed me that the placenta was not attached, which was causing me to bleed. If the placenta did not attach itself, I would lose the pregnancy. This was not good news.

Two weeks later, when I went in for another sonogram, it showed my bleeding had stopped completely. The placenta had attached itself and my pregnancy was now normal. The doctor was shocked. He said he had never seen a placenta attach itself to the womb like that. I took this as proof positive that God already had a plan for Ann. Jeremiah 1:5 says, "Before I formed you in the womb I knew you, before you were born I set you apart; I appointed you as a prophet to the nations" (NIV).

God knew everything about Ann before she was born. He had and still has plans for her. Even though my pregnancy with her would be touch and go at times, I carried her to full term. When Ann was born and I held her for the first time, I felt the same joy as I did when I held my son, Anthony, and my first daughter, Elizabeth.

4

Unexpected and Unknown

Ann was born a healthy baby. She grew just like babies normally grow, at least until six months of age. Ann was unable to sit up by herself. The only way she would sit up was if I propped her up with pillows, otherwise she would just fall over. I called the pediatrician and he told me to bring her in so he could check her out. After giving Ann a normal checkup, he assured me I should not worry and that in a couple weeks she would be able to sit up.

Ann turned seven months old and still had the same problem sitting up, though she was also not trying to crawl, and crying more often than normal. Back to the pediatrician we went.

"It looks like she has developmental delay—nothing to worry about. Some babies don't crawl or sit up until eight or nine months of age. She is on target for her weight and height. She'll be fine," He assured me.

"Why didn't Anthony and Elizabeth go through this?" I asked.

"I can't explain that," he said.

After having two other children and seeing how they both developed as babies into toddlers, I just knew in the back of my mind that something was wrong. When Ann's problems persisted through eight, nine, and ten months, the pediatrician remained adamant, "She is healthy, just a little delayed, like we already discussed. Give her time." This just did not sit right with me.

At the time, our health insurance stopped covering all vaccinations, so I had to go to the well baby clinic and get these for the kids. On one such visit, Ann was crying even more than usual and I was unable to calm her. She was still not sitting up, nor crawling. I expressed my concern about Ann to the pediatrician who had administered the vaccinations.

"Well, her head is two times bigger than what it should be," he said.

"What?"

"I said her head is two times bigger than what it should be."

"What does that mean?"

"I can't tell you why it is so large. You will have to see your pediatrician about that. All we do here is weigh, measure, and give vaccinations."

"Well, are Anthony and Elizabeth okay?"

"Yes, they are fine, normal in every way."

As I put the kids into the car, something inside me told me not to go home. I went straight to the pediatrician's office with all three kids. I said, "I don't have an appointment, but could you measure Ann's head?" They all looked at me as if I was crazy. I explained what happened at the clinic and they agreed to do it for my peace of mind. All three kids and I proceeded to the examination room with the nurse.

The nurse measured Ann's head and then simply told us the doctor would be right in—nothing more. The pediatrician came into the room, measured Ann's head, and left without saying a word. Right then, I knew something was wrong, but what? As I waited for the doctor to return, I struggled to keep all three kids occupied, and wondered what to expect. It was the longest twenty minutes ever. Finally, the pediatrician came back in and said, "I just called Grandview Children's Hospital Neurosurgery Department. You will be seeing Dr. Luke. They will perform a sonogram and CT scan, and we will go from there."

"What is wrong with Ann?"

"Her head is enlarged. From my measure of her head size, it looks like she has water on the brain."

"How? Is this why she cries so much more than normal, isn't sitting up, and not crawling? I have been complaining about all these things since she was six months old."

"I called Dr. Luke and told him what is going on. I am transferring her records to him and he will explain more," he said, totally ignoring my last question (which made me mad). Then he added, "Do not go home. Go straight to the hospital right now."

I had to forget my anger and concentrate on what needed to be done—get to the hospital. I put the kids in the car and we headed to the hospital together. The kids were hungry and complaining, Ann was crying, and I felt alone and scared. I decided there was only one thing to do: get strong and do what I had to do. We went through the drive through to get Anthony and Elizabeth something to eat. As they ate in the car, Ann cried nonstop, and I seemed to catch every red light. (Ugh!) We finally reached the hospital. The kids and I entered through the emergency room and I let them know we had to get to neurosurgery right away because Dr. Luke was waiting for us. We reached Dr. Luke's office on the neurosurgery floor but they sent us right down to get a CT scan. After the scan, we returned to Dr. Luke's office so he could share the results with us.

"I believe Ann has hydrocephalus," he said.

"What does that mean?" I asked.

"We need to do an emergency sonogram. We need to be accurate with the diagnosis. This will give us the exact cause of what is going on in her brain. You can go in with her while they do the sonogram."

If you've ever had a sonogram, you know that the technicians don't say much. When I asked the technician if they saw anything, they simply said the neurosurgeon would talk to me later. I wanted answers right then!

We went back to the waiting room to wait for what seemed like forever. Ann finally fell asleep in my arms as Anthony and Elizabeth played with the toys. As I sat there, my mind would not rest because I still didn't know what was going on. I had to rely on myself to stay strong. Finally, Dr. Luke came out and said we needed to talk, and gestured to the door. We walked to the conference room beside the waiting room. I was able to keep an eye on Anthony and Elizabeth through a huge window.

"The reason Ann has not been sitting up and falling over, crying uncontrollably, and not crawling is because she has water on her brain—hydrocephalus. Fluid is crushing her brain. She is too young to talk, so she cries to alert you that there is a problem. But there is another reason Ann has hydrocephalus. The sonogram has shown a brain tumor in the center of her brain, between the third and fourth ventricle, deep in her thalamus. It is called a left thalamic astrocytoma in her brain stem. I will explain more about the tumor, but right now I have to do emergency surgery on her and place a right VP shunt into the right side of her head to drain the hydrocephalus. We cannot wait any longer, I will see you after the surgery. Also, we will have to shave the right side of her head where the shunt has to go."

I simply said, "Do what you have to do. I will be right here."

Seven hours later, Dr. Luke came out of surgery.

"Ann is doing great. She is in recovery. I will let you see her when she wakes up. In the meantime, we need to talk about the tumor, and her surgery. We have placed a right ventriculoperitoneal shunt for Ann. We found that a thalamic mass caused aqueductal obstruction and hydrocephalus. However, there is also developmental delay you have to deal with. She needs physical therapy. We will help you get that set up. The type of tumor Ann has is called a left thalamic astrocytoma, a very stubborn type of tumor. It is also inoperable as it is in the center of her brain, right in the thalamus, in her brain stem. Children with this type of tumor usually do not make it past one year of age. Of those that do make it to one, they only live to three years of age. We will watch her closely. You will need to keep us up on any new developments, problems—anything that arises with Ann. I know I have given you a lot to digest, but I believe it is best to be honest with you."

I was in total shock, wondering what I had done wrong. How did this happen? Why did it happen? Once again, I felt so alone. I had no other family, just Elizabeth, Anthony, Ann, and I.

Anthony and Elizabeth were getting restless. I knew I had to get them home. I called my friend, Jan, and asked her to please take them home with her to let them get rest, and to bring them back the next morning to see me. I would stay with Ann. When Jan arrived, I gave the kids a hug and a kiss and they were soon on their way to her house.

As I waited for Ann to wake up in the recovery room, in the back of my mind, I kept hearing the words, "Kids with this type of brain tumor don't live past one year of age," and "sometimes they make it to three years of age." *How am I going to handle this? What am I going to do?* I wondered. Ann finally awakened. She seemed fine. Her vitals were normal and I got a smile from her. I could tell she was no longer in pain from the pressure in her head.

5

Battle Won

I settled into Ann's room on the neurosurgery floor, sat in the chair, and held her. My mind wandered a million different directions, but finally settled on my love, the love for all three of my children. It was so strong. It held me together.

In one month, Ann would be one year old. *What if she didn't make it?* I asked myself, remembering what the neurosurgeon said. *Oh, I just have to stop feeling sorry for myself. No, I am not going to give up. I have to stay strong.* (Looking back now, I wonder if my love for my children was what made me strong. Could it be the love of God, through my children, gave me the strength to persevere?) I was reminded of the word of God in Psalm 28:7, "The Lord is my strength and my shield; my heart trusts in him, and I am helped. My heart leaps for joy and I will give thanks to him in song" (NIV).

Early the next morning, the nurse checked Ann's vitals and reported no complications. Ann didn't even cry! For the first time, she was without pain. I couldn't wait to see Anthony and Elizabeth, so I called to make sure they were still coming to the hospital. Jan assured me they were on their way. In the meantime, I took care of Ann, feeding her and holding her. Then the door opened. It was Anthony,

Elizabeth, and Jan! I hugged them all. Then we began to play together with the toys in the hospital room.

Dr. Luke came in a short time later to report that Ann was doing very well, though he wanted another sonogram and CT scan to measure the tumor and make sure the shunt was working properly. They would be able to tell by the size of her ventricles. They needed to take extra precautions to be sure they hadn't missed anything. I had no problem with this because I wanted to know myself. The tests results came back just as they hoped. The shunt was working and the hydrocephalus was draining, alleviating the pressure in Ann's brain. She was smiling again, and happy.

6
Light of the World

My grandmother laid the foundation for Jesus in me, though I didn't realize this until I was older. When I was very young, my grandmother drilled into my head, "You must love Jesus." I was born and raised a Catholic and my grandmother and I went to church every holiday, every holy day of obligation (according to the Catholic church), and every Sunday. My grandmother and I would often sit and listen to the Kathryn Kuhlman radio show in her living room. My grandmother would sit in her chair and I would sit on the floor right beside her. Over and over, she would say that I must love Jesus. So even though I grew up Catholic, I was still being taught from a very young age that Jesus was the main focus.

I didn't understand it then, but I will never forget the warmth and love I felt listening to Kathryn Kuhlman's radio show with my grandmother. As I sat with her, she would always tell me stories of Jesus and how He loved us. I honestly believe now that because my grandmother taught me from a young age about Jesus, His love for me, and that I must love Him, I was able to stay strong through Ann's surgery. The fact that I received love from God through my children also helped me stay strong through Ann's surgery.

Jesus saw what we were going through and He came to the rescue, just as it says in Psalm 23.

> ¹The LORD is my shepherd, I lack nothing.
> ² He makes me lie down in green pastures,
> he leads me beside quiet waters,
> ³ he refreshes my soul. He guides me along
> the right paths for his name's sake.
> ⁴ Even though I walk through the darkest
> valley, I will fear no evil, for you are
> with me; your rod and your staff, they
> comfort me.
> ⁵ You prepare a table before me in the
> presence of my enemies. You anoint my
> head with oil; my cup overflows.
> ⁶ Surely your goodness and love will follow
> me all the days of my life, and I will dwell
> in the house of the LORD forever. (NIV)

7

Early Stages of Ann

Ann's recovery progressed very well. We were able to take her home from the hospital after seven days. We were fortunate to have an in-home therapist to help Ann learn how to walk, hold herself up, crawl, and hold objects with her hands. Yes, developmental delay had set in but not for long.

Ann needed braces for her legs. In my mind, I pictured her in big steel braces. I was relieved when the therapist said her braces would not be at all like the old-fashioned metal braces. The therapist would actually have them made from plastic in any color I wanted. Naturally, I picked pink. The braces were placed in Ann's shoes and went up to her knees, giving her support as she learned to walk again.

It was October 23rd, Ann's birthday. She had turned one year old, passing the first milestone. (How about that?) What the doctors had predicted had not come true. She had made it! We threw a birthday party to celebrate. I remember calling the doctors and telling them she was one and that we were celebrating Ann's birthday.

Ann had braces, developmental delays, and her hair had not all grown back, but none of that mattered. We were celebrating her first birthday—something I had been told would not happen. This reminded me of a scripture, Mark 9:23, "'If you can?' said Jesus. 'Everything is possible for him who believes'" (NIV).

A couple months went by and Ann's braces were shortened again—midway to the calves. Ann was sitting up and eating with utensils (fork and spoon). A few months later, her braces were shortened again, this time to her ankles (and still fluorescent pink plastic). She was able to walk with far more stability. It took a year but finally the braces came off and she could walk, sit, and live normally.

Life went on. Every six months, Ann would have an MRI and CT scan to check the size of the tumor and to make sure the shunt was working. Elizabeth and Anthony were in school, Ann was in preschool, and I was back at work. We went to church every Sunday (because I was raised a Catholic, we went to a Catholic church). I remember always going up to the altar and lighting candles for Ann. I would always hold the statue of Jesus' hands, and then pray and pray. I clung to the statue of Jesus' hands, making sure to touch the scars on them, praying and praying.

In the Catholic church, they had a healing service once a year, in October. That year, I remember the priest telling me I could put anointing oil on her during this time and that was it. This was the only time each year I could apply healing oil to her. (And I believed that?) When I look back, I wonder how I could have believed in only asking for healing once a year, but I did. I only knew the Catholic way at the time, so that's what I believed. When Ann turned two, I called the doctors again and said, "I just wanted you to know that Ann is still alive." I just loved telling the doctors they were wrong, because they kept saying she would not make it.

8

Fight for Ann's Life

At age three, Ann started to develop other symptoms, her consumption of liquids were more than normal. Blood tests came back indicating a borderline abnormal thyroid. The doctors said it could indicate diabetes setting in, though it was borderline. The doctors just advised me to take her home and watch her. If symptoms persisted, I was to call them.

At home, Ann was still not acting right. She kept drinking water and juice excessively, which had me worried. I took her back for another set of blood tests. Based on the results of these tests, the endocrinologist said they needed to run another test on her, a water deprivation test. They thought diabetes insepidus might have set in which would require a different course of action for them. I wasn't comfortable with this test, but the doctor insisted. They admitted Ann to the hospital.

At the start of the test, the nurse would come in and monitor Ann and the test every hour. As the day progressed, the nurse got busy with other patients, and did not come in as frequently as she should have. I would call for the nurse to say we needed her. She said she would be right there, but kept us waiting. Finally, after yelling at the nurse out of my anger and frustration, she came in and said Ann was fine. I told her Ann was not fine, something was wrong, but nothing happened.

At 3:00 p.m., I was certain something was wrong, and I insisted that the nurse call the doctor. Ann was not behaving normally. She had grown lethargic and begun throwing up. Immediately, we went to the nurse station and they helped me clean her up, took her vitals, and assured me that what happened was simply her reaction to the test. I wasn't buying it. (A mom knows when something is wrong with her child.) I asked for the doctor to come immediately and insisted on holding Ann in my arms. The resident and doctor on staff showed up and concurred with the idea that what had happened was simply her reaction to the test, her vitals were fine. They also said we could take her home. I said, "What? Something is clearly wrong with her." They turned, walked away from me, and began preparing the discharge papers.

As I held Ann in my arms, I walked over to the nurse station and screamed, "What's wrong with my daughter? She's too lethargic!" The nurses simply grew annoyed with me or ignored me—all except one, a nurse who was a grandmother. God sends angels in our time of need, and He sent this nurse to my rescue.

I thought Ann had fallen asleep, but in reality, she had died in my arms. The grandmother nurse noticed this first and grabbed Ann out of my arms. Holding Ann, with one sweep of her arm, she cleared her bed, called code blue, and then started trying to revive her. As I waited in the hallway, I called my friend, Jan. I quickly told her they were working on Ann, and asked her to take Anthony and Elizabeth. She assured me she was there for me. She took Anthony and Elizabeth home with her. It comforted me to know they were both safe and with their friends.

The code blue team and the grandmother nurse concurred that Ann had died in my arms, but it took them ten minutes to revive her. I agreed to her admission to ICU so they could watch her very closely. With Ann in her bed, the code blue team and I began making our way to the ICU. Suddenly, Ann threw up again while lying down, so it went to her lungs and caused her to die again. The team and I started running down the halls with Ann. All the way to the ICU, they shouted, "Code blue! Code blue!" I cannot remember ever seeing doctors and nurses run so fast, and had no idea where I got the strength to keep up with them. Not knowing what to expect, I waited outside until they came out.

A few minutes later, an ICU nurse came out and abruptly said, "Ann will be staying in intensive care. You will have to wait out here in the waiting room. If or when she wakes up, she will be a vegetable."

"What?"

Even more abruptly, she said, "She died twice. She will be a vegetable, if or when she wakes up."

"NO, SHE WON'T!"

"I'm sorry. I told you what you need to know."

"SHE WILL NOT BE A VEGETABLE!" I screamed.

"Just stay out here and we will keep you up to date with her progress."

Stubborn as I am, I refused to listen to the nurse and just followed her into the ICU where Ann was. I climbed into bed with Ann very carefully and sat cross-legged. I held her in my lap, being careful not to disturb the many tubes that seemed to be attached to her everywhere. The nurse saw what I had done, and started yelling at me, "You are not allowed in here."

"TOO BAD. I AM STAYING AND ANN WILL NOT BE A VEGETABLE!"

The other nurses urged her to leave me alone, insisting I was not bothering anyone, just holding my daughter. "Leave her alone," they said. One nice nurse made me promise to tell her immediately if I saw any changes in Ann. I said I would.

I was still a Catholic at the time. Looking back, I had no idea that I was rebuking what the doctors and the mean ICU nurse said about Ann. Had the teachings of Kathryn Kuhlman I had listened to as a young girl come back to my heart and mind? Had the Holy Spirit prompted me to rebuke the doctors and nurses?

God has reminded me of three Bible passages in regard to this situation. Isaiah 54:17 says, "No weapon forged against you will prevail, and you will refute every tongue that accuses you" (NIV). Mark 11:22-24 says: "'Have faith in God, I tell you the truth, if anyone says to this mountain 'Go throw yourself into the sea' and does not doubt in his heart but believes that what he says will happen, it will be done for him. Therefore, I tell you, whatever you ask for in prayer, believe that you have received it, and it will be yours'" (NIV). Psalm 37:4

says, "Delight yourself in the Lord and he will give you the desires of you heart" (NIV).

After my little ordeal with the mean nurse, everything calmed down in the ICU. I wondered how Anthony and Elizabeth were doing. I couldn't call them because there was no phone and I was holding Ann. I knew they were in good care because they were with Jan and her family. So I just started to pray. (I honestly don't remember what I prayed, but growing up Catholic you knew every prayer inside out, upside down, and backwards and forwards). Then I sang Ann's favorite nursery songs to her. For several hours, I prayed and sang nursery songs.

I was getting tired, but didn't move a muscle because I didn't want to hurt Ann. Finally, I said, "Okay Ann, you have had enough sleep. We have to get Anthony and Elizabeth. I have to get back to work. You and Elizabeth have to go to dance school. I have to go to the grocery store. It's time to wake up." Right then, Ann woke up and said, "Mom!"

"She's awake!" I screamed.

The nurses ran over. I climbed out of Ann's bed as the doctors rushed in and checked her vitals, shouting "It's a miracle—she's normal!

"I told you Ann was not going to be a vegetable!" I said, a bit sarcastically.

Knowing now what I know about God, I understand the Holy Spirit prompted me, though I did not realize it at the time. In actuality, I was rebuking what the nurse had said, that Ann would be a vegetable. God's Word says, "For nothing is impossible with God" (Luke 1:37, NIV). "If you remain in me and my words remain in you, ask whatever you wish, and it will be given you" (John 15:7, NIV). Through my study of the Bible, God's Holy Word, I know in my heart that Jesus was there all the time because I put my trust in Him. Jesus gave us the victory because of my faith in Him. Praying in God's Word starts opening the door, and our faith in Jesus is the key to opening the door fully for answered prayer. Hallelujah! God is truly amazing.

I asked the doctor why this had happened to Ann. He said the nurses were very busy and had not monitored Ann's water deprivation test adequately. Her electrolytes fell below normal and she died. By the grace of God, Ann came back to normal. As to the nurse assigned to Ann, because of her mistake, she lost her license to practice nursing. (A mom knows when something is wrong with her child.)

As for the diabetes insepidus, doctors ruled it out. Though the doctor reports said Ann was borderline diabetic, after subsequent blood tests, there was no sign of it. This is all God. He took the diabetes away. Praise God!

9

Another Mountain to Climb

Life went on as normally as it could and a few years passed. I was divorced by then, and raising Elizabeth and Ann on my own. Anthony decided to live with his dad. I worked two jobs to support our family, and on top of that, drove the kids to school, dance school, sports, and doctors. Ann was still living with the brain tumor and was progressing normally.

Living on my own with the kids, and working two jobs was a struggle, but a happy struggle. Life started to get better for all of us for about three years, until Ann, now ten, became ill again. We were driving in the car and she began holding her head and screaming, "My head hurts! I feel something rushing in my head." She just kept screaming, getting louder and louder. I said, "Ann, stop! I know you have a headache, but stop!" We reached a stop sign and she began crying uncontrollably. I looked at her again, saw the pain in her eyes, and just knew that something was wrong. I picked up Elizabeth and drove Ann to the hospital. (Again, listen to your child when they say something is wrong).

On the way there, I called the neurosurgeon to alert him to what was going on. After I hung up the phone, I just began to pray and ask Jesus to help us because I had no idea what was going on. I recalled what my grandmother taught me, "You must love Jesus and pray." I prayed.

The doctor met us in the emergency room and ran an emergency MRI. He alerted me that the tumor had begun to hemorrhage. Though it was a small hemorrhage, he warned me that if the bleed continued, he could do nothing for her. Her head would fill up with blood and kill her instantly. If they plugged up one hole where the tumor was bleeding, another would start. If they plugged up the next hole, another would start bleeding. It would be a vicious cycle, and unable to be fixed. (At least this was the doctor's report.)

Ultimately, the doctor told me the only thing we could do was go home. Ann would need to lay still for a couple days—no school, no anything. I had no vacation time available at work, so I had to find someone to stay with Ann while I worked. (As you can imagine, I called every hour to see how Ann was doing!) I kept Ann out of school a full week and we returned to the neurosurgeon for evaluation.

The neurosurgeon reported that Ann seemed to be doing fine. He said they could not do another MRI right away because the blood was fresh and they couldn't tell if it had stopped, so if they did it right away, they would likely get a false reading. We scheduled it for three months later. Since Ann seemed to be doing well, at least from the doctor's point of view, he advised us to go back and live a normal life. Ann was allowed to go back to school.

Three months later, they gave Ann an MRI and found that the bleeding in the tumor had stopped. This was truly a miracle. We thanked God and our lives soon went back to normal.

Exactly one month after the MRI, Ann began holding her head and screaming again. All I could hear her say was, "Stop the pain, Mom! It feels like blood rushing through my forehead! Stop the pain, Mom." I got a sick feeling in my stomach and just froze.

Once again, Elizabeth, Ann, and I got into the car and drove straight to the emergency room. I did not even bother to call the neurosurgeon this time. Upon arrival, I told them what happened three months before, and that the same symptoms she had then were happening again. As I filled out the paperwork and held Ann, I looked at Elizabeth and fear gripped me inside. I didn't know what to expect. My stomach was turning. I felt all alone. I had no one to call to come and be with me during this time. It seemed as if the paperwork was never-ending. I knew I had to pull myself together and get strong for the girls. I finally finished the paperwork and they took us to the emergency trauma unit.

The neurosurgeon came down and we went right upstairs where they did a CT scan and an MRI. His report was grim, "I am sorry to say Ann's tumor is bleeding again." This time, before we left the hospital, I reached up and grabbed the neurosurgeon's arms (all 5 feet 3 inches of me, grabbing the 6 feet tall neurosurgeon), saying, "Why won't you help us? Why won't you operate and get rid of the tumor? Why are you letting this happen?"

He removed my hands from his arms and said, "Cindy, look at me." He held out his hands in front of me, palms up and said, "God did not give me steady enough hands to operate on Ann. Ann is in God's hands. You have to believe, Ann is in God's hands! I'm sorry I can't operate. I will not have this on my conscience. You know the tumor is inoperable and she has lived longer than any child with this type of tumor. Take her home. She is to be out of school for the rest of the year, no activities. She is to rest. She can do homework she missed at home with you. We will do another MRI in 3 months. I'll see you then unless you need me before that." He left me standing there, numb, and headed back to his office. The girls and I left for home.

I was in shock. Though I had heard everything he said, I just couldn't understand why all this was happening. This time, the bleed from the tumor was large and it took a toll on Ann. She lost feeling in her left side completely, both upper and lower extremities. The next day, I went to Ann's school and told them what was going on, that she couldn't go to school, and that she would be homeschooled. The teachers and principal worked with us and were very understanding. She was homeschooled for the last part of the year. I talked to my boss and got my schedule changed so I could be there for Ann and Elizabeth. I called a friend and asked her to stay with the girls when I had to work. So with my schedule rearranged and the girls taken care of, we went on with life as normally as possible.

Still in shock and unsure what to do, I went to the first Catholic church I found open. I lit candles and knelt at the altar right beside the statue of Jesus. After praying, I touched Jesus' hands again and held on to them, knowing deep down inside I needed to do something to save Ann's life. I started mulling every avenue I could think of to help me. Even though I was praying, I was still trying to fix the problem on my own. At that time, it was the only thing I knew to do. I prayed, but I was counting on myself to fix the problem, not God. Knowing what I know now, when I face a difficult situation, I seek God for the answer. Amazingly enough, the answers are in the Holy Bible, and found in spending time with God, talking to Him through prayer. As I let God take charge and work through me as a partner to solve the problems, He will guide me to victory...as long as I will let Him. As I put my full trust in Him—not only His Word, but put full trust in Him and that He will take care of the situation—He will indeed do just as I have asked.

God loves every one of us so very much. He does not want us to go at life alone. God knows the end from the beginning. Our belief in His Word and promises, our unwavering faith, and our belief that He can do what He says He can do —all of these determine how the situations we face will turn out.

10

Looking for Answers

The next day I called Dr. Luke, our neurosurgeon and told him what I was up to. I couldn't just sit around and not do anything to help Ann. He told me I could do what I wanted, he would not be mad, but reminded me that Ann was in God's hands. I got Ann's medical records and proceeded to contact all the well-known neurosurgeons who saved kid's lives. I contacted Dr. Jones who used the Gamma Knife surgery. After reviewing Ann's records, Dr. Jones said he absolutely would not do it. He said the surgery was too dangerous for Ann and he would not have it on his heart that Ann died because of his surgery. He urged me to go back to Dr. Luke because "he knows what he is doing." (Dr. Luke travels the world to save kid's lives—other kid's lives, not Ann's.) I wasn't satisfied.

Then I contacted Dr. Blake, also very famous. After transferring Ann's records to him, he wrote me back to say, "I am sorry. I will not do the surgery. I would not be able to live with myself, knowing the consequences of the surgery. The tumor is inoperable. I decline to do the surgery." I was not happy.

I had heard Canada had good doctors. They simply told me go back to Pittsburgh, as they would not operate, the surgery was too dangerous, and the tumor was inoperable.

So there I was, a single mom, fighting for everything in my life and my child's life and coming to a dead end, totally unable to do anything. I didn't know what to do. I talked to a couple friends and they all told me to listen to what the neurosurgeon said, "Ann is in God's hands." I was not satisfied. I still felt that I should be the one to save Ann's life. After a couple days, I called the neurosurgeon, Dr. Luke, and said, "I've come up with nothing, you are still her neurosurgeon, and I will listen to you.

11

Missing Piece of Life Found

A month later, a friend of mine introduced me to a new church. It was all right but not what I was looking for. In truth, I really didn't know what I was looking for. We went to another church and really liked it. They welcomed us as if we had been there before. The girls and I had attended this new church for about a year...yet something was missing.

One friend kept telling me to read the Bible. I protested that it was all Greek to me. Every time I read it, I don't understand it. I read the words but they have no meaning. The next Sunday, we went to church and, out of the blue, a couple said they wanted to give me a present. It was the *Jesus Study Bible* (NIV). (God works in mysterious ways.) "We heard how you were having trouble understanding the Bible and we feel that this will bless your life and your children's lives," they said. I thanked them, but kept wondering why they gave me a Bible. I didn't even know them. Still, I was thankful for the gift. That night I started to read it and to my surprise, I could understand what I was reading. The words were not Greek to me!

About that time, life got harder and I knew that something was missing from our lives. I still didn't know what to do. I called the pastor of the church we were attending but there was no answer, so I left a message. He called back to tell me he had a meeting first thing in the morning, so he couldn't meet with me. I insisted I needed to talk to someone. He said he would call me after his meeting and then we could set something up for later in the week. Well, I wasn't satisfied, so I got up early the next morning and went to the pastor's office before his meeting. I needed to talk and didn't care if he had a meeting. I refused to take no for an answer.

When I got to his office, he said, "Last night, something told me I wasn't going to my meeting today. I asked God why, but He didn't tell me. Now I know why. Come in, sit down, and let's talk." I poured my heart out to the pastor and he listened intently. After I finished talking, the pastor said, "Now I want you to tell God everything you told me. Are you willing to be saved and accept Jesus Christ as your personal Savior? Are you willing to ask for forgiveness of all your sins?"

"Yes, but I can't talk to God, you have to—you are the pastor."

"My child, you need to talk to God. He is the only one who can help you and meet all your needs."

"But I've learned from growing up Catholic that only the priest can go to God, and then He will forgive us."

"My child, you are not in a Catholic church anymore, you are in the house of God. We believe in the Gospel of Jesus. We believe in the Word of God, the Holy Bible. You must go to God yourself and ask for forgiveness, pour out your heart to Him, accept Jesus as your personal Savior, and He will guide you. I will leave you alone. I want you to talk to God and tell Him what you told me."

I was so scared. This was something I had never done before. So I knelt down and started to talk to God. I cried and told God everything that was bothering me and asked for forgiveness for all my sins. Then I accepted Jesus as my Lord and Savior.

Half an hour later, the pastor came back and said, "How did it go?"

"I did it, I talked to God! I told Him everything and accepted Jesus as my Lord and Savior. I feel peace for the first time."

"Now I know the real reason I didn't go to the meeting. Are you okay?"

"Yes."

"I'll see you and the girls in church on Sunday!" he said.

I gave him a hug and went on my way. When I got home, I felt complete; I had found the missing piece in my life. Looking back, God was with me all the time, I just didn't know how to let Him in. My grandmother laid the foundation. "You must love Jesus," she had said over and over again. She would say, "It's time to listen about Jesus," and we would listen to Kathryn Kuhlman's radio show. She would sit in her chair and I would sit right beside her on the floor, but at that time I didn't know what I was being taught. Still, somehow I remembered Jesus.

In Revelation 3:20 (NIV), the Bible says: "Here I am! I stand at the door and knock. If anyone hears my voice and opens the door, I will come in and eat with him, and he with me."

I thank God that the pastor didn't go to his meeting and that I let Jesus into my heart. God knew what I needed and He was right on time.

12

Complications Set In

Just as I started to get our lives back together and on track with God, another serious battle began. Every day, Ann began suffering out of control migraines. She had blurred vision, felt like throwing up, felt blood rushing in her head, and had pressure pounding in her head like a sledgehammer. She felt as if her brain was being squeezed. She cried constantly and started to miss school. I knew it was time to call the neurosurgeon, Dr. Luke.

I rushed Ann to the hospital and a CT scan and MRI were done. Everything looked fine. Her ventricles were small, there was no bleeding and no tumor growth, but Ann's symptoms were a sign that her shunt might be malfunctioning. The neurosurgeon did a shunt tap to measure the pressure in her head and make sure the shunt was functioning properly. They pulled fluid out of the shunt and sent it off to the lab to see if there was any type of infection in it. The pressure was fine. I brought Ann home.

Three days later, the neurosurgeon called me and said, "Get Ann in here now! Her lab results are positive for infection. Do not waste time!" They did another emergency shunt tap, and this time the lab results came back negative for infection. (God wins again!) The doctors decided the migraines were the result of a tumor and that we should try pain medicine to help her. They also advised us to see a neurologist to help her with the pain. This was the beginning of another battle.

13

A Tug at My Heart

In the meantime, one Sunday in June, Ann received Jesus as her Lord and personal Savior. I found out Joyce Meyer was going to be in town. I told the girls I wanted to go hear her and they went with me.

Ann's Account

I got saved on a June day in 2001. My mom told me about a speaker she listened to, Joyce Meyer, and invited me to go with her to hear her. I hated being at the house, plus the convention was free—how could I pass this up? My mom took time off from work just to go to it. My sister Elizabeth, her two friends, Marcia and Candice, my mom, and I all went to the convention.

I don't even remember what Joyce Meyer was talking about now, but I know God tugged at my heart. I walked up to the stage and gave my heart to Jesus. Amazing! I felt change in me that was strange. I didn't understand what it was. I got saved! I remember telling my friends about it and they just laughed at me. (Whenever my friends laughed, I remembered how blinded I had been to Jessica in third grade, when she told me about her getting saved.)

After this, my mom, Elizabeth, and I tried to find a church—church hopping, as I like to call it. At work one day, my mom was listening to a praise and worship CD when one of the nurses told her about her church. It was Vine Assembly of God, the church we go to now. We went first to a Sunday night service. But this Sunday night service was different. It was youth mission night, when students who have gone on mission trips share their experience with the church. The students had just returned from El Salvador and all expressed that the kids down there had stolen their hearts. They got to hold the children in their arms, play games, sing songs and teach them about Jesus in creative half hour presentations. They also got to dance (and their dances were awesome!). I couldn't understand the words to the songs—they were in Spanish—but they were awesome.

I so desire to do that one day—to go on a mission trip and share love with kids who do not know what true godly love is. How I long to see just one display of affection for these kids do such a work that they are changed instantly, have smiles on their faces, and know there is hope. How wonderful for these kids who live such burdened lives to simply be kids for a while with none of the worries that poverty and hunger bring. Though I am not so much a clown person (so the teens who love to do that would have to handle that part), but I would do very well with balloon animals! I had never heard of a mission trip before, and I was so inspired by all I had heard and seen that I wanted to go to the youth ministry. At the time, I was a brand new believer, still very young in my walk with Jesus as Lord and Savior. I just knew that I needed to go to youth group.

I first met Pastor Shawn, the youth pastor, at the youth mission night service. I was so struck by the fact that he was just as excited as the students about the mission trip. He was so proud of his students and just had an amazing quality about him. Every student listened intently to him, leaning in to learn more from him. Many students from the youth group were there that night because of the mission team's return; they were eager to hear what had happened. At the end of the service, I went up to have someone pray with me. I asked a girl named Lily to pray I would be able to go to youth group, and that my mom would get off work on Wednesday nights to take me there. Amazingly, she was able to and I was able to go to youth group!

When I went on my first retreat, I was a bit scared because I had never really been away from my mom for a weekend. I went anyway. My roommates were so sweet. After that, I went to every Wednesday night youth group service, just searching for more of God because, as Pastor Shawn always said, God wants us closer to Him. I told a number of people in the youth group that I had a brain tumor, since birth. Pastor Shawn and the youth leaders would often pray for my healing. Little did I know what would happen next.

14

When the Doctor Gives Up

Ann and I went to see the first neurologist, Dr. Charles. The doctor was frustrated because he didn't know how to handle the severity of the migraines. He had given Ann medicine to stop the pain, but to his amazement, they did not work. After many calls to him, each time he told me to bring her in so he could try something else. This went on for at least two months. Still, Ann suffered migraines 24/7 with no relief in sight.

Dr. Charles said, "I'm sorry I can't help your daughter. The pain medicines I am giving her should have helped, but they have not." The neurologist at the hospital discussed Ann's situation with the board of neurologists and still, nothing. His suggestion was that we see another doctor, very famous (rated #1). He said this doctor worked with patients who suffered migraines and, "He also does TV appearances. That's how good he is. He has helped many people. I'll make the appointment for you because he has a waiting list and it is very hard to get in to see him."

The first appointment was great. Doctor William reviewed the MRI scans and discussed Ann's history with us. He explained that the tumor was pressing on the "number 11" part of the brain. He compared this part of the brain to a gas pedal and explained that normally, when people take pain medication, this pedal lets up and they are out of pain. This was not the case with Ann. Ann's brain tumor kept the gas pedal pressed, preventing it from letting up, causing her migraines to be severe. He said he knew of some medicines that could help her and suggested she try one of them. He wanted to see her again in one month and told me to call if I needed him in the meantime.

Ann's battle continued, though we felt as though we had made some progress because this doctor had actually explained what was going on in her brain. Still, as great as it was to know more about what was going on in Ann's brain, evidently this was not the entire answer. Ann's migraines got worse, so we went back to see him, explaining that the medicine was not working. He urged us to try something else, so we did. The cycle of medicines that did not work continued. The more Ann complained and we tried to talk to the doctor about her symptoms, the more frustrated he became. Finally, he threw up his hands and said, "I can't help your daughter. I give up."

"Why can't you help her?" I asked.

"I don't know what to tell you except that I can't help your daughter. There is no hope for Ann."

I just looked at him in shock. As Ann and I left the office, the nurse asked us if we wanted to make another appointment. I said NO, very strongly. Never had I known or heard of a doctor giving up on his patients.

I called Dr. Luke who had referred us to the neurologists, and told him what had happened. He said we could try other neurologists, and promised to look into others for us and let us know what he found. I agreed.

Even though Ann had a brain tumor, hydrocephalus, and migraines, we tried to put our lives back together. We all went on as though the brain tumor did not exist. We led a positive life, resolved that everything was going to be alright and Ann would live a normal life. I continued to get Ann to all her doctor appointments and dance school. My work life continued on as well.

15

Another 1,000 Steps

In January 2004, Ann, Elizabeth, and I all got the flu. Though Elizabeth and I recovered in two weeks, Ann did not. She remained sick. Something inside told me that something was wrong. I immediately called the neurosurgeon. (Why, I don't know.) I explained to Dr. Luke that for over a month, Ann had been sleeping too long, very lethargic, throwing up, not eating, and just not her normal self. I did let him know that I had taken her to the pediatricians and they confirmed she had the flu. I also mentioned that Elizabeth and I had recovered from the flu, but not Ann. He told me to bring her in for a CT scan. It was worrisome to me because of her history: left thalamic astrocytoma, headaches, vomiting, and hydrocephalus.

I took her to the hospital to get the CT scan and MRI. The CT scan showed her shunt was functioning normally and there was no change in her ventricles—they were normal-sized. The MRI showed worsening of the left thalamic astrocytoma, now with extension in the midbrain, and that there was now right thalamic involvement. And this takes us back to the beginning of the book, where the battle gets more intense. We did not realize this could happen.

16

Gift of Life

I was working at an office job Monday through Friday, 8 a.m. to 4 p.m., and worked some overtime on weekends if I wanted to. I took a day off to get Ann an MRI and CT scan. The results showed that her tumor had grown. I was upset and did not know what to do. I reached out to God and asked, "What do I do now?" Dr. Luke said we needed to get a biopsy of the tumor to see what we were truly dealing with. Although the tumor was benign, it was still life-threatening for Ann because of its growth and the pressure it placed on her brain in the thalamus, which controls the body. Dr. Luke said we needed to act fast and get the biopsy done as soon as possible. I called and requested a couple more days off from work, after explaining what was going on. They were not happy, but I really didn't care. My main concern was Ann. When we got to the hospital for Ann's biopsy, she was scared and started to cry.

In the hospital the night after her biopsy, a nurse named Nadine came into Ann's room and talked to her while giving her pain medication.

"How long have you had this tumor," she asked.

"Thirteen years," Ann answered.

"You know there is a divine reason it has grown now. There is definitely a divine intervention coming for you with this brain tumor. I will keep you in my prayers. You will make it. Just keep believing." Ann and I were just amazed at how God put people in our lives at just the right moment to give us a word of encouragement. Could she be an angel sent by God?

Dr. Martin came in and told us the results of Ann's biopsy, saying the results confirmed the tumor was benign, though what it was doing to her brain would be fatal for Ann. They had to act fast. After going before the pediatric tumor board and the adult tumor board, they concurred that the best way to treat the tumor was through surgery. Not regular surgery, but Gamma Knife surgery, which was a form of radiation.

I had spoken previously to our neurosurgeon about Gamma Knife surgery. He had been against it, deeming it too dangerous. So how could a surgery that was too dangerous for Ann be okay now and not before? "This surgery is the strongest of the radiations and the one we are most hopeful will kill the tumor," Dr. Martin assured me. "We hope and pray the tumor will respond to the Gamma Knife surgery. This will be a very stubborn tumor. There is still the possibility she will hemorrhage. I do not want to do anything to hurt her—I want to save her life." I wondered if he realized that he would not be saving Ann's life, and that it was through the grace of God that Ann would be healed. I told him that I would not do anything until I called Dr. Luke, who had followed her case from birth and knew her history like the back of his hand.

The biopsy had been done at a different hospital than the one Ann normally went to because the former could not do the biopsy. So the results came from a new doctor and hospital. I just broke down and cried because it was so hard to see my daughter go through with this. How was I to make the right decision from what I already knew? This was all extremely emotional and draining. But I know that through the grace of God, I would be able to get through this with Ann.

I immediately called Dr. Luke and discussed the results of the biopsy with him, telling what Dr. Martin had advised, Gamma Knife surgery. He said he would discuss this with a board of neurosurgeons to see which would be the best way to go. He felt we needed more opinions.

As I reached out to God, praying and believing His word that Ann would be healed, I kept hearing Him say, "Trust me. I am the Alpha and Omega." I can't say I wasn't nervous or upset, but there was a peace with me that was unexplainable. God also spoke to me and gave me this verse: "May the Lord repay you for what you have done. May you be richly rewarded by the Lord, the God of Israel, under whose wings you have come to take refuge" (Ruth 2:12, NIV). Then He gave me another verse, "I will not die but live, and will proclaim what the Lord has done" (Psalm 118:17, NIV).

God is an awesome God and I knew in my heart I would have my little girl back again. Right after that, He gave me the verse, "I am the good shepherd; I know my sheep and my sheep know me" (John 10:14, NIV). Jesus' interest is in his sheep, whom he enables to have life to the full. Life is

Jesus' gift and He is the life. Jesus is the light of the world. "For with you is the fountain of life; in your light we see light" (Psalm 36:9, NIV).

I returned to work while awaiting the results from the second meeting. A woman I worked with, Maria, told me that her son had gotten all the youth groups and churches in the area to pray for Ann. During her biopsy, 3,000 kids had prayed for Ann because of Maria's son. In, God's Holy Word it says, "Again I tell you that if two of you on earth agree about anything you ask for, it will be done for you by my Father in Heaven" (Matthew 18:19, NIV).

17

Decision of Doctors

After the second meeting with the board of neurosurgeons, Dr. Luke called me to say he needed to speak with me in his office immediately. I told my boss I needed to leave to meet with the neurosurgeon and off I went, picking up Ann from school on the way to the doctors' office. We sat down with Dr. Luke and he proceeded to tell us that according to the biopsy, Ann had a pilocytic astrocytoma of the thalamus. The tumor was benign, but ultimately fatal because of what it would do. The tumor was in the center of Ann's brain, on the thalamus, between the third and fourth ventricle, and it was growing at a rapid pace. The tumor was already pressing on her brain and killing some of the nerves in it. Two were dead completely. As the tumor grew it would apply greater pressure on Ann's brain, which would prove fatal, over time.

This type of tumor was usually removed by surgery, but in Ann's case this would not be possible because of where it was located. It was very stubborn and would be very hard to treat without surgery. Such tumors did not usually respond to radiation, but there was a chance it could. They were considering three types of radiation: Gamma Knife, laser surgery, and chemotherapy. They needed to find the best type of radiation and the safest way possible to treat Ann. The beginning of next week, they would call me in to discuss it, and then I would have to call the insurance company to get authorization to pay for the treatment. The plan was to act very quickly and get her back into the hospital ASAP.

The results came back from the second meeting. They had decided Gamma Knife, though a very strong type of radiosurgery, would only kill part of the tumor. It would not do the job it was supposed to do and might even cause the tumor to explode, which would kill Ann. The pediatric tumor board voted on IMRT (intensity modulated radiation therapy) radiation five days a week for six weeks straight, fifteen minutes a day. Though it was an older form of radiation treatment, it would be the safest way to go. The tumor had branched off and grown into the top of Ann's brain stem, which controlled her body, and her brain was swelling. The IMRT would kill the tumor and not hurt Ann. I asked what would happen if it didn't work. He said we would cross that bridge if and when we got to it. When he asked us if we wanted to try it, both Ann and I said yes.

I asked the doctor again what his thoughts were on IMRT radiation and why there had been so much controversy in the meeting. He said the conversation had centered on the fact that the tumor was life-threatening and inoperable. They had decided IMRT would be the lesser of two evils. He promised he would monitor Ann's progress, and we would meet once a week to discuss it. I said, "Okay, let's try this."

18

God Working Behind the Scene

The next day, I met with my boss to discuss everything and how extremely important it was. Unfortunately, she was not cooperative at all. Ann's treatment appointments were scheduled for 4:30 p.m., every day. Since my workday ended at 4 p.m. each day, the hospital was forty-five minutes away, and I had to pick up Ann before driving there, I would have to get off work earlier than 4 p.m. each day. I offered to come in and work an hour early each day to make up the time. She said no, flat out no. She said I could leave at 3:45 p.m. each day and that was the best she could do. There was no talking to her. I quickly learned every shortcut around traffic and back roads from work to Ann's school, and to the hospital. Talk about cutting it close every day! But we did it. Between working, getting Ann to radiation treatments every day, taking care of Elizabeth and taking her to a friend's house, my life was extremely busy. We did this for six weeks.

During this time, I truly knew that God was our only answer and continued to press into God's Word and go to church and took Ann to youth group. I received an encouraging note from a friend who attended an intercessory prayer meeting in Ohio.

Ann,

There was a woman sitting next to me this morning at the intercessory prayer meeting. I don't know her, but she shared this note with me after I put your name on the prayer list and we prayed for you. Believing for your miracle!

The woman, Kathy, wrote:

Sunday night in my church, a prophet was ministering. She asked me to come forward. She told me I had healing in my hands. I was also blessed to receive a healing anointing in Alabama. I know this is from God. After the prophecy, I went back to my seat and God told me there was a person with a brain tumor. If I would pray for her and believe for her healing, it would be done. I prayed, not knowing who I was praying for, and God told me that the tumor would not take life. Today, when I heard about you, I knew this prayer was for you. Believe with me that you are "loosed" from the tumor and the effects of it. I believe life for you.

In Christ,

Kathy

In honesty, Ann, Elizabeth, and I had been scared. Ann and I had often cried together. We began to realize how blessed we were. From the onset of the tumor at Ann's birth, God had been with us. Ann had endured a rough thirteen years, but she had overcome all the obstacles set before her because of the tumor. All these miracles had happened because of the grace of God. We were so thankful. In realization of all this, Ann, Elizabeth and I decided to take the positive approach.

God had been with us all the time (and still was). We were looking at all the blessings God had given us, not at the problem. We were standing firm on His Word and His promise. He would do what He told us He would do. He had given us a church we called home, where we could feel His presence. We knew that He had heard all of the prayers of the church, as well as mine, Ann's, and Elizabeth's. He had given us a wonderful church family we could talk to when we were scared, just needed friends, or needed to rejoice in the Lord. God had given Ann a wonderful youth pastor, Pastor Shawn, who taught the students to never give up and to stand strong on God's Word. He cared so much for his students. It was truly amazing, how the light of Jesus shined through him all the time as he encouraged them with his words, and shared God's love with them. He was always there for Ann.

I knew God would make a way for the doctors to help Ann.

19

A Distance I Could Not Reach on My Own

We really thought radiation would be the answer, but soon realized we were actually facing another battle.

During the radiation, Ann kept getting worse. She would complain to me and I would let the doctors doing the radiation know. They just kept saying, "Let the radiation work." Ann's complaints only grew stronger. Another week went by and Ann's condition began to worsen. Her headaches raged, she was very nauseous, her vision was blurred, she had double vision, and she was experiencing coldness in her legs due to her blood not circulating well. One doctor advised us to have Ann try a very strong painkiller as she continued with radiation. Needless to say, it did not work. Ann just got worse.

As Ann experienced these problems, I never forgot God. I was very upset though and speaking only to Ann, Elizabeth, the doctors, Pastor Shawn, his wife Jen, and God. I kept praying and trying to read the Bible, but was getting nothing out of it. I kept asking God if He was mad at me. I kept seeking God because He was my only source to get through the things I was going through. As I was driving Ann to youth group one evening, on the windshield of our car I saw the words TRUST IN GOD, in big bold letters. I was amazed. Then I heard God say, "Read Daniel in the lion's den." I wondered what that story had to do with me. He said again, "Read Daniel in the lion's den." I did and saw it was all about trusting God. He never left me. I had been so upset; I had allowed the flesh to rule me. But God had broken in and was making everything better.

Midway through the six weeks of radiation, I had had enough. I called Dr. Luke and told him everything that was going on with Ann. He said he could do another MRI, but he was afraid we would get a false reading. I was insistent that Ann could not keep living as she was, and we needed to do something. He said he would schedule an MRI, and then we would discuss it. I agreed. We went for the MRI, but it turned out just as Dr. Luke had predicted, he could not get a clear picture. He urged us to continue with radiation and promised to check in on Ann at the end of the week to see how she was doing. After discussing this, we agreed.

Ann endured another bad weekend, health-wise. Her headaches were excruciating, her legs were severely swollen, her face and neck were swollen even more, her eyes were crossed and she lost her vision twice for periods of ten minutes at a time, and she was very tired. I noticed a huge lump the size of an orange on the back of Ann's neck. I called Dr. Luke and he just told me to watch her closely. UGH! On Monday, I called off work and took Ann to see Dr. Luke without an appointment. In a very strong voice, I said, "Someone needs to help my daughter, *now*! I don't have an appointment, but you will see her *now*, and I will *not* take no for an answer!" After Dr. Luke examined Ann, he looked me straight in the eye and said, "Ann needs a lot of prayers, hope, and faith in God. Continue with the daily radiation and pray. Ann is in God's hands."

That night at church, they held a special healing service, so I took Ann. Ann and I stood on our belief that she was already healed, but in part, *Ann had begun to believe the negative words of one of her doctors:* "Only radiation can heal Ann. If it doesn't work, we can try another radiation. If that doesn't work, well, you already know this is fatal. There is a chance that Ann won't ever live a normal life."

I told Ann that she could not focus on the flesh, and that she had to keep believing and not to give up. I told her she had overcome so much by the grace of God, she couldn't give up now— I certainly was not giving up. I believed Ann was healed.

When we got home, Ann fell asleep. Around 12:30 a.m., she woke up crying because her head hurt so bad. I reminded her again of the healing scriptures we often quoted, and we prayed. We just kept fighting back with the Word of God. I knew that Ann was scared, and kept praying in faith that she had been healed, and for Jesus to just wrap His arms around her and hold her. I knew she was losing the strength to fight back—she was getting weaker. I shouted out, "God, we need a miracle, in the name of Jesus!" She finally fell asleep around 1 a.m.

The next day. I got a call from a dear friend who asked how Ann was feeling. I explained what was going on. She said, "Well, guess what? A friend of mine, a pastor, called me this morning. She awoke suddenly at 12:30 a.m. and felt led to pray for Ann, which she did until 1 a.m." I told her that was the exact time Ann had woken up in pain the previous night, crying. At 1 a.m., Ann had finally been able to get to sleep, in peace. "God is healing Ann!" I exclaimed. He had seen her hurting, came to her, and helped her. *Wow,*

God is good! Thank you, Lord, and please continue healing Ann.

Radiation continued and Ann kept getting worse. The doctors would not listen to me and kept urging us to just keep doing the radiation, and that she would be fine.

"Look at all the complications with Ann now," I said. "I know she is on medications to stop the complications of the radiation, but look at her. She is getting worse! Why can't anyone see this?"

"Fine," the doctors and nurses of the radiation department said. "We will take her off all medication except the pain medications. But she will have to live with the side effects of the radiation because she can't take the medicines."

"Don't you realize the tumor is not responding to this stupid radiation and making everything worse?" I said.

Unmoved, they said, "You have to finish the radiation. When six weeks is up, we will know if it worked or not."

"Why won't anyone listen to me? Are you all so blind that you can't see what's going on?"

Since the radiation was done at another hospital, Dr. Luke was monitoring her from afar. Ann was under the care of the doctors and nurses in the radiation department. Dr. Luke knew what was going on because I kept calling him, though because of the circumstances, he couldn't act anymore.

We had to fully rely on God.

20

Struggles of the Journey

During this time, I was still working, struggling emotionally, and physically drained. But I kept putting on a happy face and saying I was strong when I was not. On the way to work, I thought of how much I wished I could be a full-time mom and take care of Ann and Elizabeth the way they deserved to be taken care of. But of course I couldn't; I had to provide for them.

Ann and Elizabeth are both great girls. They earn high honors in school, don't get into trouble, are loving and caring, respectful, and help me by cleaning the house and carrying other responsibilities in our household routine. Even when Ann was weakened from all the symptoms of the tumor, she still tried to help.

I remember thinking: *I wish my grandmother were here. I really need someone to hold me...to help me. This is so hard to handle by myself. Yes, I have friends but they all have families of their own to take care of. So here I am, all alone.* Then after a few minutes of reflection: *Oh, I just have to stop pitying myself. We made it this far; we will make it further. Get strong!*

Ann called me one day at work and said, "Please look up Exodus 14:13, and Exodus 13:14 in the Bible. These scriptures have been put on my heart, but I can't remember which one." She knew I always carried my Bible to work. So I stopped working and looked them up. I read: "Moses answered the people, 'Do not be afraid. Stand firm and you will see the deliverance the Lord will bring you today. The Egyptians you see today you will never see again. The Lord will fight for you; you need only to be still" (Exodus 14:13-14, NIV). I also looked up the other verse which read: "In days to come, when your son asks you, 'What does this mean?' say to him, 'With a mighty hand the Lord brought us out of Egypt, out of the land of slavery'" (Exodus 13:14, NIV). I typed these verses and made a copy of them. Before the next radiation appointment, I gave the verses to her. She smiled ear to ear. They restored her positive attitude. I could tell she was starting to feel better; she was happy. (Isn't God great?)

That night, Ann called me from her bed. She was unable to walk due to all the pain and swelling in her legs. I just told her to keep praying and believing and God would get her through this. This was an extremely difficult time of struggle for Elizabeth, Ann, and I financially, emotionally, and physically. Watching Ann go through this was very hard, but as I told her then, "God only knows why we are going through this. One day we will know the reason. But for now, we have to keep our trust in God."

At Easter service, God spoke to me and reminded me to speak in faith; to say that Ann was healed, even though we couldn't see it yet. The Bible says, "Now faith is being sure of what we hope for and certain of what we do not see" (Hebrews 11:1, NIV). I love God so much. Though there are times in life that are incredibly painful, we truly are blessed because God is with us every step of the way.

Once again, I called Dr. Luke and told him Ann was still having the same problems, but they were getting worse. "Do something, please," I begged. Once again, he said we could do another MRI, but we would likely not get the correct readings on the tumor. "Just do it," I said. "Ann knows her body better than anyone and we both want it done." And once again, the results came back unclear. Though extremely frustrated, we finally finished the six weeks of radiation.

Ann attended school part time, though Elizabeth was in school full time. We were happy to have Ann home with us instead of in the hospital. I kept on working. Every week I called Dr. Luke to update him on Ann. He advised us that we were able to get an MRI done that would give us a correct result.

I called off work and we got Ann an MRI. We were surprised when Dr. Luke reported the results: no change. *Now* what? After everything we had been through, Ann worsening, my workplace giving me a hard time, shipping Elizabeth off to a friend's house, our lives turned upside down, there was no change. I insisted that they do another MRI; there must be a mistake. Dr. Luke assured me that the test results this time were clear and there was no change. "She is in God's hands," he said again.

That night as I was praying, I said to God, "God this is me, Cindy, Ann's mom. I am not ready to give her up yet. Please don't take her. She has so much to live for and I don't want her to die. Please don't take her!"

I heard God reply, "This is not her time to go. Trust me."

"I hear you loud and clear. Please promise me that before it is her time, you will tell me so I can prepare for it," I said.

"Yes," I heard God say. "When it is her time, I will let you know. Now is not the time for her to go. Remember this. I have spoken."

Radiation is finally over! The girls had one month more of school. My boss finally stopped giving me a hard time. Ann was doing a little better. We were trying to get our lives back to normal, even though we knew the MRI results were not encouraging. We were still going to church, and the girls were going to youth group. We all tried to stay happy and enjoy life as best we could.

They did another MRI two months later and it too came back showing no change. On top of that, Ann had not fully recovered from the radiation. She still had blurred vision, crossed eyes, double vision, and lost her vision completely from time to time. Her headaches were worse. I was not sure what to think or do, so I just kept trusting in God. I tried to keep a positive attitude and enjoy the summer with the girls, went to work, got caught up on bills, continued the doctor appointments, and went to church, of course. This was our life. We survived May and June, even though Ann still faced her health issues. We made it through.

21

Keeping the Faith

Soon, it was July. Throughout Ann's life, she engaged in many battles with the tumor, and overcame every one of them by the grace of God. God's hands have been on Ann from birth and He never let go. Even though we couldn't see them all the time, His hands were always there. God was always there. Even when the battles got tough and we wanted to give up but did not, He always gave us a word of knowledge from the Holy Bible. We did not expect the next battle we faced.

In spite of Ann's continuing recovery from the radiation, we had just reached the point where we were living a semi-normal life. I called Dr. Luke and told him Ann was not behaving normally. He recalled talking with me just two days before, and going over her progress, and that there was no change from what we discussed the last time.

I replied, *"I understand that Dr. Luke, but that was two days ago. This is today.* Ann has taken a turn for the worse. I don't call you with a complaint about Ann's condition unless it is real. Why won't you listen to me? Ann's headaches are worse, she is lethargic, wants to sleep all the time, and doesn't want to eat—plus she is feeling nauseated. She has blurred vision, double vision, has lost her up gaze, and loses her vision completely from time to time.

She is experiencing body tremors, and her legs are stiffening up."

"Two days ago, she did not have all these symptoms," he replied. "Bring her in for an emergency MRI and CT scan. I'll meet you in the emergency room."

Dr. Luke examined Ann, but didn't want to do anything until he reviewed the results of the MRI and CT scan. "Take her home and I will call you with the results. Don't worry," he said. How do you tell someone not to worry when their child is going through something like this?

I took Ann home and Elizabeth and I tried to keep her up as much as possible, because we didn't want her to fall asleep and not wake up. Elizabeth wanted to go to a friend's house, so we drove her there. The next day, I went to work and Elizabeth took care of Ann. A couple days passed and still there was no phone call from Dr. Luke. I began worrying, wondering what to do, and whether or not to call. I reassured myself, *If there was anything wrong or different, he would have called me by now.* I went to work while Elizabeth stayed with Ann at home. That's when the call came. I will never forget it. It was noon on a Friday, and it was Dr. Luke.

"How is Ann?" he asked.

"She hasn't changed. She is still the same as when we last talked," I said.

"I have never made a call like this before..."

"What are you talking about?"

"The reason I haven't called you back is because I have met with the board of neurosurgeons here at the hospital.

I have also taken Ann's records to other tumor boards in different cities and states, trying to get help in making the right decision what to do. No board can come into agreement on Ann's treatment."

"What did the tumor boards say?"

"There was a lot of disagreement, but most of the doctors said that surgery was the best bet. The tumor is growing aggressively—grown considerably, to the size of a tennis ball with new tumor growth cells. It is growing across the brain. Some of the neurosurgeons are saying to do surgery and others are saying no. Cindy, Ann's tumor is taking over her brain and her time on earth is getting more limited than we thought. There is no easy way to say this...but you told me always be honest with you. You and I have known each other since Ann was born and she is a fighter..." he said, his voice cracking as he struggled to find the words.

"Dr. Luke, what are you trying to tell me?"

"You have until Monday morning at 8:00 a.m. to make the decision...to either have the surgery...or watch Ann die."

"What?" I screamed. "How can you ask me to make a decision like this? I am a single mom, no family, by myself, and I have to make a decision like this? How do I make the right decision? How can you call me and ask me this?" I cried.

"I know you are going through a lot, but you are on a very strict time limit here. You have until 8:00 a.m., Monday to make the decision. There is a surgery I know of that is possible, and it is our only hope right now. With this surgery there is a 1 percent chance of Ann dying on the table, 1 percent chance the tumor will hemorrhage, 15 percent chance of paralysis, 25 percent chance of personality change, a 50 percent chance her eyesight will remain the same or get better, and a 90 percent chance the headaches will go away. You and Ann can come in so we can discuss the surgery in detail in my office. I will expect your call, Monday. Goodbye."

How was I supposed to work today after receiving such a devastating phone call at work? I was hysterical and everyone else was at lunch, so there was no one to talk to. I just sat at my desk and cried. Finally, I pulled myself together and went to talk to my boss, Susan.

"Susan, I need to talk to you in private."

She looked up from her paperwork with a disgusted glare and said, "What now?"

I explained to her the phone call I had received from Dr. Luke, and that I would need time off.

She threw her pen on the desk, stood up, and said, "Cindy this company does not have room for single mothers who have sick children, you're fired."

Totally shocked, I screamed, "You can't do this to me."

"This is a blue collar state and business owners can fire and hire anytime we please."

"I'm going to the owner's office right now. This won't happen!" I went to see the owner and recounted what had happened. It did not go well.

"I'm sorry, Cindy. Whatever Susan says, I agree with it. She runs the company for me; I just own it. You may leave now."

First, I received a devastating phone call and then I was fired. *Wow, what next?* I cleaned out my desk, took all my pictures with me, and left. As I was leaving, everyone kept telling me to sue the company. I was thinking about a far bigger decision I had to make. One more decision and I felt like I would break. I couldn't take it anymore. Enough was enough.

I left the parking lot and drove home, crying all the way, hitting every red light due to busy Friday afternoon traffic. *Don't people realize I need to get home to my daughters? Why is there so much traffic?* Finally, I reached home. I saw Ann and asked her to go get something to eat with me. Elizabeth was upstairs, so I shouted up to her that when I got back with Ann, I needed to talk with her, and for her not to go anywhere.

22

Why? (Ann's View of That Day)

I remember the day like it was yesterday. Mom picked me up from the house and said we needed to go get something to eat and talk. I was not feeling well. I could tell mom had been crying. Mom took me to get something to eat. We went to the drive through, got our food, and drove to the grocery store parking lot. I just knew something was wrong. We parked the car and Mom began to cry.

"What's wrong? Am I dying today?" I asked.

"There's a possibility of surgery."

"What's the surgery?"

"Resection of half the tumor."

"What's the chance I'm going to die?"

"One percent."

"Let's do it. You said you would do anything to save my life."

"But Ann, you don't understand all the risks." She then proceeded to tell me all the risks.

"There is a risk of paralysis, personality change, cognitive delay, coma...even death." We discussed only the death part.

"Mom, I don't want to die. I know normally we would pray about it, but there isn't enough time." Mom rambled on about what Dr. Luke said the surgery would do, but I interrupted her. "I am all for it, Mom. God is a lot bigger than the risks. I am trusting Him to save my life. Mom, you said that you would do anything to save my life."

"Yes, but I am not losing my happy Ann."

"You won't. It's only a 25 percent chance. God won't let it happen."

"So you want to go through with it?"

"Yes, I do. Nothing is going to happen."

Well, at least I hoped nothing would happen. *My personality can't change—God wouldn't let it. I can't become paralyzed. How would I get to my room? I'm not going to die. Maybe I should talk to God now, this is scaring me so much. Dr. Luke said he couldn't do surgery and now he can. It doesn't make sense. He already said all possible surgeries wouldn't work. The tumor is inoperable. I don't understand how he just, like, invented a surgery and is going to try it out on me. I know Pastor Georgia gave me the verse, "I will not die but live, and will proclaim what the Lord has done" (Psalm 118:17, NIV). I will stand on this verse, but I am scared. What if God does take me home? I don't want to leave my mom. Last week, I was told I had six months; now it has turned into a weekend. I don't understand what you are doing God—I don't understand at all. Why do you want me dead so badly?* I didn't understand it at all.

Why had mom told me this right when I was about to eat? Forget eating. I was sick to my stomach and feared I would throw up.

"Are we going to meet with Dr. Luke before the surgery so we can talk this over?" I asked.

"Yes, on Monday. He will perform the surgery on Tuesday, if I call him back and say yes."

I promise you, my life flashed before my eyes. You know how people say that just before they were in a crash or bad accident their life flashed before their eyes? Well, that happened to me right then.

Mom drove us home.

Then I told God something I had promised I would never say to Him: I told Him what I was never going to do. I told God I wasn't going to do anything with my life, and now that I only had until Monday, I was never going to graduate high school—I wasn't even going to graduate middle school. If I did survive surgery, I feared I would never be able to walk again. If I couldn't walk, I wouldn't be able to drive, get a job, dance—nothing. I thought I would never get a real boyfriend, get married, have kids—none of this. I would rather die than be paralyzed. I thought there was no way I could live like that. I feared I would lose all my friends. One of my friends, Landon, is in a wheelchair, but he has been in one for a while. Maybe my friends would accept me like they accept him? Maybe it won't be that bad. No, I cannot become paralyzed!

We finally arrived home. I didn't want to deal with any of it right then. *Maybe if I pretend this isn't happening, everything will change.* (That is how it happens in movies isn't it? Ugh!) *Maybe if I go to a friend's house I'll forget about all of this.* I assumed Sutton and Monica were busy and decided to go to my friend Natalie's house.

I stayed at Natalie's for about an hour, and told her and her parents what was going to happen. They said they would pray for me, which was nice. I just never thought I would be going through this, especially at age thirteen. I said I would call them after my surgery, or the day after. *It's a ten-hour surgery, I'll call them the day after it. That will be better,* I thought.

I hoped mom wouldn't have to wait alone during my surgery. I knew God would be there, but I hoped she would have another friend with her also.

Maybe this is all a bad nightmare, I will wake up in the morning and it will be all over, I thought. Ha ha! I could only wish.

23

Trusting God's Hands

I could not sleep that night. I just kept replaying in my mind what Dr. Luke had said. The risks of the operation weighed heavily on my mind, especially the one regarding the personality change, and the risk of becoming mean. Ann had always been a very happy girl, always smiling, not a care in the world, and full of life. She was always singing, caring, and never mean. How could I let her have the operation if it caused her to become mean? What was I going to do? I was surely not going to let her die, but I refused to do anything that would cause her to become mean. Though there were other possible consequences of the operation, the personality change was not letting me go. I thought to myself, *This is extremely serious. I have to make the right decision.* The three of us, Ann, Elizabeth and I, discussed this all Friday night.

Late that night, I cried out to God, "How can you let this happen to Ann? If we have the operation, she will become mean. God, you know Ann has always been happy, never ever mean, always caring, and full of life. Please don't let her become mean. If I don't allow the operation, she will die. God, why was there no warning—no nothing? Why? Don't let this happen!" Suddenly, I heard God's voice and can honestly say He was mad at me. In a very strong, stern, loud voice He said, "I AM THE POTTER!" His voice was loud (I mean, LOUD). *I'm in trouble...God's mad*, I thought to myself. He spoke again, "I AM THE POTTER! READ THE BIBLE." I was so afraid because I knew I had hurt God by looking at the circumstance and listening to the world, and not Him.

Minutes later, I started looking for my Bible. I always sleep with my Bible, it's like my security blanket, but I did not have it with me that night. I looked and saw it on my nightstand. I abruptly got out of bed, picked it up, and looked up "potter," finding Isaiah 45:9-12. As I read the passage, I immediately broke into tears, repenting and apologizing to God. I asked Him to forgive me for believing the doctor's words over His words. I talked to God, expressing how I felt and He gave me peace. Then I prayed, "Ann is in your hands, Father, and I am going to trust you. We will go ahead with the surgery."

24

Listening from the Heart

Monday morning came and I couldn't wait until 8 a.m. I called at 7:30 a.m. and told Dr. Luke we would do the surgery, and that Ann and I were on our way to see him to discuss everything. We met with Dr. Luke and he explained to us that there had been significant interval increase in the size of the left thalamic tumor. It had crossed midline to involve the right thalamus and infiltrated the dorsal brain stem right greater than the left. There had been significant expansion of the posterior midbrain, though there was also extensive enhancement in the left side. The tumor had grown extensively. Without the surgery, the tumor would just take over Ann's brain and kill her sooner than expected.

He emphasized that not all the neurosurgeons on the brain tumor board agreed with performing the operation. Then he recited the risks once again: 1 percent chance of Ann dying on the table, 1 percent chance of the tumor hemorrhaging, 15 percent chance she would be paralyzed, 25 percent chance her personality would change, 50 percent chance her eyesight would remain the same or get better, 90 percent chance her headaches would go away.

Then he described the operation. "I want you both to know exactly what I will be doing. I will cut out the new tumor growth, however, I will have to be very careful because it is in the cerebellum also. I have to leave the tumor in the brain stem, because no one can touch the brain stem. Basically, what I will do is resect the tumor."

Ann brought up exactly what I was thinking, "But I thought you said God hadn't given you steady enough hands to operate on me."

Dr. Luke looked Ann in the eye and said, "Now is the time to operate and God has steadied my hands to perform this operation on you. I want to save your life, with the help of God. I am not here to hurt you."

Ann looked at me and said, "I'm ready, Mom."

"Okay," I said.

I asked when the surgery would take place. Dr. Luke said we couldn't waste any time, we had to do it the very next day. Then I signed all the pre-op paperwork as he went over it with me, Ann had to get blood work done, and we needed to get a few prep things done. He told us to be back at 8:00 a.m., and "Ann, Cindy—trust God. I'll see you in the morning."

We left Dr. Luke's office and went to get everything done that needed to get done. When we got home, Elizabeth was waiting for us. We told her everything, and she asked if she could go to her friend Autumn's house until we got back. I agreed.

"Mom," she asked, "will you or Ann be mad if I don't go to the hospital with you?"

"No sweetheart, I understand. This is hard for all of us. Just keep your phone on and we will keep in touch that way.

Ann understands that hospitals are not for everyone. It's a hard thing to go through. I'm going to get mine and Ann's stuff ready for the hospital and then let's get something to eat before Ann has to stop eating before surgery."

Elizabeth and Ann were always very close, so it was very hard for Elizabeth to see Ann go from living a normal life to being so violently ill. Elizabeth said, "Ann, you're a very strong person and you are going to make it. Remember, we have movies to watch and a lot to do when you get out of the hospital. I can't spend the summer without my sister, so come home quick. Got it? Good!"

After I had gotten everything ready for the hospital, I sat quietly at the table, drinking my coffee. My life, everything the girls and I had gone through, all flashed through my mind. *Am I really strong enough to handle this surgery tomorrow?* I wondered. There was no one around to talk to and I needed honest answers. There was only one person I knew would answer me, but I wouldn't get a voicemail from Him—God. I said, "God, you and I have walked through every storm together; you never left me. I know you are not going to leave me now. I need to remain strong in you. Hold me in your arms. I also ask you to hold Ann and Elizabeth in your arms during this surgery. And God, I also ask you, from my heart...please be in the operating room with Dr. Luke, Ann, and the other doctors and nurses. Guide Dr. Luke as he performs the surgery. Take charge of the surgery, God, and loosen your holy angelic forces to be in the operating room also. In Jesus' name I pray.

25

Not Sure (Ann's Thoughts Before Surgery)

Tomorrow I go in for surgery. There is a one percent chance I will die. This is what I keep repeating to myself. God, I know Pastor Shawn isn't going to come to the hospital. If he does, I will know for sure I am going to die. No, he is on a mission trip. Wow, I never thought that at thirteen, I would be dealing with these thoughts—that maybe I am really going to die. I am so scared of going through this surgery. When mommy told me about the surgery, I was so confident, but now I just don't want to do it. I am seriously scared out of my mind. I told Natalie this was no big deal. I can't look like I am scared in front of my friends.

The surgery is going to take ten hours—I think that's what Dr. Luke said. What if he gets tired and messes up? I have to sleep with these stupid blue things, circle stickers, so they know where to drill in my head. The MRI people put them on me. I am scared I am going to lose them in my sleep. I just need to go to sleep and not think of what might happen. "Real quick, God; thank you for Ben being so sweet and giving Elizabeth the cup of coffee to give to me. Too bad I didn't finish it. Mom can though."

God, help me.

26

God Works in Mysterious Ways
(Ann's Words)

At 5:30 a.m., Mom woke me up to leave for the hospital. Amazingly, none of the stickers fell off me last night. All I could think was that I just wanted to get the surgery over with. The night before, I think God held me. Now I needed a for real sign from God.

It was so hard to brush my teeth since I always swallow the toothpaste at the end. As I brush, I think that the previous night was probably the last in my room.

As mom drove me to the hospital, she played the praise and worship music tape we both loved. I thought for sure that once we reached the hospital, I would ask her to take me home, that I would insist I did not want to go through with the surgery. The verse Pastor Georgia had given me, came back to my mind, "I will not die but live, and will proclaim what the Lord has done" (Psalm 118:17, NIV). I had been standing on this...but now I did not want to go through with this surgery. I was scared...really, really scared. I didn't want to die.

We finally reached the hospital. I had my white bear Miss Fallon (my sixth grade teacher) had given me. I was glad to know Belle would be with my mom at the hospital.

Elizabeth hates hospitals, I understood that, so she would not be there. I would talk to her as soon as I woke up. Even walking into the hospital confirmed for me I did not want to go through with the surgery, and I let mom know it.

"Mom, take me home, I want to die," I said, crying.

"You are not going to die."

"Take me home, now. I want to leave."

"Honey, come here. You are not going to die, and we are going through with the surgery. We have to be strong. We are going through this together."

As I bawled my eyes out, I promise you, an angel came down from heaven. A lady came over to me who had obviously seen how scared I was, and said, "Hi, my name is Virginia."

"Hi, I'm Ann."

"Is this your first surgery?"

"No. I had shunt surgery as a baby."

"May I pray for you?"

"Yes, you can pray for me."

As she prayed for me, I promise, God sent peace through me like a river. I calmed down and we finished registering. As I turned to thank Virginia for praying for me, she was nowhere to be found. As fast as she had appeared, she had disappeared. We never saw her again.

We had to register in one hospital before finally registering in the other, Grandview Children's Hospital. Thankfully, they were connected by a bridge. Belle was already waiting in the waiting room. She had gifts. Then Marcia came, another dear friend of ours, bringing even more gifts. I remember Marcia gave me a ginormous sticker book. I love stickers.

The nurse called us back and began interviewing me. She asked if I did drugs, smoked, drank alcohol, or if I was pregnant. Thankfully, I could answer no to all those questions. They made me change and then put me in a bed. They transported me upstairs, with mom walking beside me. Once upstairs, they said there would be a short wait. I just wanted to get it over with.

I turned on the television and there was nothing good on. Mom held my hand and let me know everything was going to be fine, and encouraged me to stay strong. I could see she was scared too. As we waited, Pastor Tim came in where I was waiting and prayed with mom and I. Pastor Tim was filling in for Pastor Shawn. *What a sweetheart.*

Pastor Shawn was away on a mission trip in Philadelphia. He had told me before he left that he would be praying and thinking of me. Pastor Tim was there for another family, but had wanted to stop by and see me too. Just before they gave me shots and put in my IV, Pastor Tim left.

Minutes later, mom and I heard someone say, "Knock-knock!" (as I was in a curtained "room," without a door). It was Pastor Shawn, my youth pastor! He came in and asked to pray with me. I asked him how he got here—he was supposed to be on a mission trip. He said he wanted to see me before I went in for surgery. He had left the mission trip and traveled a long distance just to pray with me.

Unfortunately, the night before I had somehow concluded that if Pastor Shawn came to the hospital, I was going to die, for sure. (You know those shows on TV about people from out of the area coming to see someone in the hospital—then the person dies? That is why I thought this—I'd watch too many of those shows.) So Pastor Shawn came in and I thought for sure I was going to die.

Pastor Shawn tried to keep me happy and told us about the mission trip. Finally, after they told us they were ready for me, Pastor Shawn, mom and I prayed together. After that, I told him goodbye, that I loved him, and to tell the youth group goodbye and that I loved them too. "Don't forget to tell Jen (Pastor Shawn's wife) I love her too!" He said he would and then he left. When they took me back to get me a series of shots, I told mom goodbye and that I loved her. "Tell Elizabeth and Anthony I love them, and goodbye." I seriously thought I was going to die. Mom said, "I love you too. I'll see you when you wake up." I honestly thought to myself, *You will see me in heaven.*

27

Miracle of Miracles

Dr. Luke came to see me right before surgery and said the nurses had Ann ready to go and he was ready to do the surgery. He didn't see any reason for complications and said he would be very careful and only do what he had explained to Ann and I. He urged me to stay strong and I said I would. After he left, I grabbed my purse and Bible and went to sit with Belle in the waiting room.

In the waiting room, Belle offered to get me some coffee. I thanked her but declined. I just wanted to sit and think, and pray. I tried to read my Bible, but couldn't. I remember praying and crying out to God, and remembered what He told me, that He was the potter.

This had to be the longest ten hours, ever. When you watch the clock, time moves so slowly. Finally, I couldn't take the suspense any longer. I went to the nurse and asked how the surgery was going. She assured me that if there were any problems, she would let me know. From all she knew and had heard, everything was going well. I told her I would not be leaving the hospital, that I would stay in the waiting room, and that I wanted to know anything and everything. Though she urged me to go to the cafeteria to get something to eat and drink, I insisted I could not eat at a time like this. Belle came over and offered to go to the cafeteria to get us coffee and get me something to eat. I agreed.

Alone in the waiting room, I opened my Bible and said, "God, right now I don't know what to read or how to pray, but I know Ann is in your hands. Please be in the operating room with Ann and the doctors and nurses. I trust you to bring my little girl back to me."

I looked up at the clock and saw there were two hours more to go. Belle returned with coffee and food. I thanked her and gave her a hug. I drank a little bit of coffee but didn't eat. A few minutes later, Belle said she had to leave to pick up her kids from school, but that she didn't want to leave me alone. I assured her I would be alright, that I understood, and she needed to do what she had to do. "We will be fine," I said. After Belle left, I felt very alone. I had my Bible and my coffee.

The next time I looked up at the clock, I saw there was one hour to go. I began pacing the floor.

Finally, ten hours was up. I went to the nurse's window again and said, "Okay, ten hours is up. Where is Dr. Luke? How is Ann? Why isn't Dr. Luke out here talking to me? It's been ten hours." She said she would go and find out what was going on and left. She returned a few minutes later and reported that the surgery was taking a little longer than they thought. Ann's blood pressure had dropped, so it was taking a little longer. She promised to keep me updated. I returned to the waiting room realizing I just needed to pray harder, which I did.

An hour later, Dr. Luke came out to sit and talk with me. He said Ann was fine.

"We got the spread of the tumor out of her brain, both the right side and the left side. We had to be very careful around the cerebellum. Amazingly, most of the tumor came to the top of the brain stem. We were able to get rid of the tumor on top of the brain stem without hurting Ann. However, we could not get the center of the tumor in the brain stem. She did very well in surgery, except for one time when her blood pressure dropped. She came through with flying colors...oh, and there is one more thing I have to tell you."

I looked at him and said, "What? What?"

"I know how picky Ann is with her hair. But the resident started to shave her head in the wrong place. I stopped him in the nick of time, but I know she will be upset with that. Tell her it will grow back, and I apologize."

I couldn't help but give a trace of a smile. "Okay, I will tell her. When can I see her?"

"I have her in ICU recovery right now, in a private room. I thought you would like that better. You can stay with her there. The nurses will call me when Ann wakes up and I will check her to make sure she is okay."

I asked if he would be leaving after the surgery, but he said he planned to stay until Ann woke up. I was relieved to hear that. I called Elizabeth, Pastor Shawn, and Belle to tell them surgery had gone well, that Ann was out of surgery and in recovery, and that I would call them when she was awake. I told Elizabeth I would not be home that night. She said if she could spend the night at Autumn's house, she would be fine. I assured her it was fine with me if it was okay with her parents.

"Mom, how are you doing?" she asked.

"I'm worn out, but okay. I love you, Elizabeth. I will stay in touch with you. Try to have some fun tonight. Oh, and when Ann is in a regular room and can have visitors, I will come and get you and bring you here to see her."

"Mom, you know I hate hospitals!"

"I know, Elizabeth, but I just want you to know that you can come and see her."

"I'll let you know," she said, pausing slightly. "Tell Ann to hurry and get better because we have a lot to do. Besides, I need my sister home."

"I'll pass along the message."

After the call, I settled into the hospital chair in Ann's private room and waited for her to wake up. Ann's nurse came in and introduced herself to me, Aria. She said she would be taking care of Ann until she woke up. Then they would move her upstairs to her regular room. I was okay with that but asked her how long it would take before Ann would wake up. She said that Ann was heavily sedated, so it could take awhile.

I had thought the surgery took forever, but waiting for Ann to wake up seemed even longer. Every hour, Aria would come in and get Ann's vitals. Nothing changed, though she assured me everything was going as planned.

Just before midnight, I heard, "Mom, mom, mom...where are you?"

"Right here," I said, "I never left."

I called Aria and told her Ann was asking for me, she was awake. Ann grabbed my hand, squeezed it and kept saying, "Mom!" Aria came back from calling Dr. Luke and said she needed to check Ann's vitals again. Ann kept trying to touch the bandage on her head, and I kept telling her to keep her hands down, that it was just the bandage. She said she felt sick. I asked Aria if she had heard Ann talking. Aria said she did and that she would take over from there, so I moved to the other side of her bed.

Aria bent down to look in Ann's eyes and as soon as she did, Ann turned her head and vomited on her. It was classic. You always see this in movies, but this was real life. I know it's not funny when someone throws up on another person, but it was amazing how the nurse told me to move and then she was the one who got thrown up on—even hitting her in the face. The nurse wasn't happy, but I couldn't help but laugh (then apologized for doing it). I was tired, but as the Bible says, "the joy of the Lord is our strength" (Nehemiah 8:10, NIV).

Dr. Luke came in and checked Ann as Aria went and got cleaned up. He said Ann was normal and responding just as he thought she would, and that she was going to be fine. The next morning they would move her upstairs and he would see her soon after that. He left soon after.

I thanked God and praised Him because I had my little girl again and He had kept His promise to me. (Isn't God great?) It was midnight, so I couldn't call anyone with the good news until the next morning. So after all the excitement, Ann and I just talked for a little while before she fell asleep, holding my hand. I actually got an hour's sleep and was at peace.

We serve a mighty God and He is so awesome in keeping His promises to us. He is a faithful God.

28

When the World Says No, God Says YES

Morning came and we were moved up to a regular room. Ann was responding normally. She had so many visitors, cards, balloons, and stuffed animals, they filled the room. Ann was smiling and laughing, her personality had not changed. Praise God!

Four days into her hospital stay, Dr. Luke said he needed to talk to me.

"Cindy, I am putting Ann into a rehabilitation facility."

"Why? She's my daughter and I can take care of her."

"No, she needs therapy and you can't do it on your own."

"Yes, I can," I insisted.

"Okay," he said, "try and help her walk."

"Watch me," I said.

I tried to get Ann up to walk and she couldn't. She was paralyzed. *Another battle. Here we go again,* I thought. I had to admit, he was right. Dr. Luke had already called the facility and they were set to transfer Ann the same day. Then he said he had something else he needed to tell me. I just looked at him and pleaded with him not to give me any more bad news.

"I can no longer serve as Ann's neurosurgeon," he said. "The board was against Ann's surgery, and warned me not to do it. I knew I had to save her life, and I followed my heart and didn't listen to what the board said. I listened to God. So now, I have to step down and am no longer her neurosurgeon."

I didn't know what to say. I was shocked.

"Can I talk to anyone for you," I asked.

"No, they won't listen, their decision is final. You have to finish taking care of Ann. I will be fine, though thank you for your concern. I will never forget Ann. She's a special girl and God has a purpose for her in life."

29

The Grace of God

I called Elizabeth and told her what was going on. She asked how long we would be in the hospital. I said I wouldn't know until I got there and talked to them. I told her that as soon as I got Ann settled in the rehabilitation hospital, I would go and get her. She told me to call her then.

We arrived at the hospital, and after filling out all the paperwork, they admitted Ann and assigned a room. The doctor came in and introduced herself, "Welcome, I'm Dr. Linda, and I will be taking over Ann's case. I want you to understand that Ann is paralyzed, and she will be here for a very long time. It is possible she may never walk again—"

"Excuse me," I interrupted, "Ann will walk again, and we will not be here long."

"I know it's hard for you to accept—"

"Stop right there. Ann will walk again. She might be paralyzed now, but not for long. I know firsthand, when God starts a miracle He completes it. He doesn't do a halfway job. He always sees that His Word does what it sets out to do."

Shortly after this, Ann started therapy. Little did we know that God was working behind the scenes, because the first week, Ann was walking with a walker. By the second week, she was walking by herself with no walker, with a steady gait. It was a remarkable recovery. I saw Dr. Linda and had to tell her, "See? I told you she wasn't going to be paralyzed for long, and that she would walk again."

Everyone at the hospital was talking about Ann, that she was a miracle—a walking miracle. The buzz spread throughout the hospital. Ann was doing so well I asked to take her to youth group. Dr. Linda asked how many kids would be there, and I said there would be about 100. She said Ann could go, but she would have to go in a wheelchair and use the walker just for protection, so she wouldn't lose her balance and fall. I agreed outwardly, but inside, I knew differently. We did take the wheelchair and walker with us, and drove to youth group. We had not told anyone we were coming. It would be a surprise.

Ann's Account

When I got to youth group, I have to admit, I was nervous because I heard the doctors say I needed to be extra careful and not have a lot of people around me. My two friends came with me to be my "assistants" and help me out. I rolled in and Pastor Shawn was stunned to see me. Before the service, I got to tell the other people in the youth group about what happened and they were so happy to see me. It made me feel really good to know that people actually care rather than just say it and not mean it. During youth group praise and worship, he gave me a special shout-out before one of the songs. Smiling ear to ear, he said, "That's Ann...the miracle!" I was pumped. I never had a shout-out like that!

After service, as usual, Pastor Shawn was talking with the students. He didn't know I could walk, since I had arrived there in a wheelchair. So he didn't expect what I had planned. I called him over and he told me how happy he was that I was there. I put my wheelchair in the locked position and started to get up. He was thrown off guard since he didn't know I was walking yet.

"Sit back down," he insisted, concerned. "You aren't supposed to be walking."

"Yeah, I am," I said.

Then I walked across the room and we both shouted praises to God. He knew God *could* and *was* going to heal me, but I think he was struck by the wow factor, because I was not supposed to be walking so soon. I sat back down and rolled out into the lobby of the church to show another one of my pastors that I was walking. He said, "Praise the Lord!" After that, we went back to the rehabilitation hospital.

Amazingly, I was released from the rehabilitation hospital in twenty-eight days! I was supposed to be there much longer than that.

30

God's Truth Is Marching On
(Ann's Words)

School was starting up again. I was allowed to go to school for a half day, though I was still under the doctor's care and had to start out slow. I didn't have to take many classes, but I still had to study.

In November 2004, we went for an MRI to see how everything was. The MRI revealed the tumor was...*gone*. Praise God!

However, in March 2005, after I went for an eye appointment that raised some concerns, we learned the tumor had grown back. This was not what we wanted to here. It was even in the same place, the brain stem, and inoperable. However, I was living a normal life. My mom and I said together we would fight this and put our trust in God.

I graduated the eighth grade on time in 2005, with the rest of my classmates. Even though the tumor had come back, I still went on my first mission trip, to Denver, Colorado. It was amazing! On our way there, two of the leaders and I got into trouble for going to a different part of the airport. Ha-ha! Good times. The mission trip was so amazing. Even I, a girl with a brain tumor, could do the work of God. How much better could it get?

31

Miraculous Life of Ann Continues

Ann's Account

It was time for school to start up again. I was in high school. My mom had to meet with the teachers and guidance counselor because I had to have an IEP (Individualized Education Program). Due to the surgery, I still had some cognitive delay.

Everything worked out. I attended full days in high school, though I never achieved perfect attendance. I tried to live a normal life. I did average work in school and survived ninth and tenth grade. I had an IEP throughout high school.

Then came the eleventh grade, and I started preparing for college. Some of my teachers and counselors told me in so many words that I wasn't going to be anything in life. One of my counselors even told me to just go to community college, because "a girl with a brain tumor will never get into any other college." (This struck me as funny. After all, counselors *are* supposed to encourage you and not put you down, right?)

Well, guess what? I proved that counselor wrong (and was only too happy to do so).

I believe in miracles, so by the grace of God, I got into Valley Forge Christian College. (When I did, I recalled my eleventh grade English teacher telling me, after I wrote an essay incorrectly, that it would be a miracle if Valley Forge accepted me.) As everyone else fretted over their college applications, I had already been accepted. WOO-WEE! At my high school graduation, as I walked across the stage and grabbed my diploma, I knew that had it not been for God, I could never have done it.

Over my high school years, I went on many more mission trips. We went to New Orleans, Nicaragua, and Denmark, to name just a few. I never thought I would be going on mission trips—I had thought I was going to die. The mission trips were totally amazing. Just to be there for others to help them meant so much to me. I remember holding the little kids in Nicaragua. It felt so good to give them the love they longed for. Oh, there were so many precious memories from all the trips that I will never forget. Eventually, I became a youth leader.

During high school, God called me to become a youth pastor. It's wild, how God has a calling for everyone, even one with a brain tumor. In spite of my medical problems, I kept busy throughout high school with youth group and mission trips. Yes, the brain tumor existed, but we kept living a normal life, as though it wasn't there. At times, it was very hard for me because I had migraines 24/7 and there was nothing any doctor could do about it. I began getting sick again from time to time. Even though we never gave up, it was still hard.

As I prepared to start college, I still had to see many doctors. My mom did a lot of research to try and help me with the migraines, but every time she came up at a dead end. I remember the day she got calls from three different doctors and they all told her the same thing.

Cindy's Account

I was driving home when I received a call from the first doctor who said, "I'm sorry, there is nothing anyone can do for your daughter."

"I will be the judge of that," I said. "I have a call in to another doctor as well. I will see what he says."

Then the second doctor called me to say, "I looked over Ann's medical records and honestly, I can't help her. There is nothing anyone can do." I was furious at this point. I just hung up the phone.

Finally, I received a call from the third doctor who said, "I'm sorry, I can't help your daughter. She just has to deal with her migraines and being sick."

"What kind of doctor are you?" I said. "It's real what she's going through, you see, and yet no one wants to go near her. She doesn't have the plague you know!"

"I'm sorry," he said, "but no doctor can help your daughter. She is just going to have to suffer." I was so mad, I hung up the phone without saying goodbye.

I stopped the car in the middle of the road and cried out to God, "God, you told me if this was Ann's time to go, you would warn me ahead of time so that I could prepare for it. What do I do now? Ann is getting ready to go to college, she has gone on mission trips, and now no doctor wants anything to do with her. What am I supposed to do now,

God?" I wasn't expecting a quick answer, but I heard God say: "Jesus healed many with natural ingredients from the earth. Read the miracles of Jesus." Right after this, a car came up behind me. (It was weird, how there were no cars on the road except mine until God spoke, and then cars were back on the road.) I started driving again, anxious to get home and read the Bible.

I found out that Jesus healed with natural herbs (mud, water in the Jordan river, etc.), so I told Ann and Elizabeth what happened and said I was going to contact a herbologist to see what they had to say. We were all in agreement. I also prayed about it and was at total peace with it. That night I heard God say, "I will heal Ann through herbs—no more surgeries." I knew I was on the right path now.

I found a herbologist and took Ann's blood test results to her. Much to my amazement, she told me that because of the radiation treatments they had administered to Ann, all her organs were damaged and her blood was not good. She said, "I can help her if you will let me." I went home and talked to Ann, telling her what I had found out. She said, "Let's get the herbs, Mom." But what about all the medications Ann was on? She and I both agreed she would quit cold turkey and flush the medications down the toilet. We would start the herbs the next day, putting all of our trust in God, no more medicines.

I let the doctors know our choice to pursue herbal treatments for Ann. They didn't give me a clear idea whether they agreed with it or not. I knew I was on my own. About six months later, we had new blood work done on Ann. *Every* organ in her body was perfectly normal, from kidneys to liver to heart to lungs, and so on. The herbs had obviously worked. Though the migraines weren't gone, that was all Ann had to deal with, so we were happy. She didn't need the herbs any longer, so she was off them by the end of her first semester of college. Ann thanked me for listening to God and starting her on the herbs.

32

Laughing in the Devil's Face

Ann was in college and doing very well with her studies. Her IEP carried over into college, but it was still an adjustment.

Ann's Account

Since I was in Philadelphia and my home was in Pittsburgh, the opposite side of the state, it was really nerve-racking, being away from mom. It took a full semester for me to feel at home while away at college, but I made it. I knew I was studying to be a youth pastor and doing the work God called me to do. Each semester got easier, and college truly became my home away from home. My mom and I talked every day. (Thank God for cell phones!) I still dealt with migraines every day, but I was not sick all the time as I had been through high school.

I passed my freshman year, then sophomore year. Each year, I would go back for an MRI just to make sure there was no new growth in the tumor, since it had grown back in March 2005. Each time, they told my mom and I that everything was good, despite the tumor still being there. The doctors would say they were sorry that nothing could be done for the migraines, but on the bright side, the tumor had not grown.

I finished my junior year and began my senior year. Very soon, I would officially become a youth pastor. Throughout my college years, I had been part of Audience of One, our college human video team, and started my own ministry, Precious Gems, which ministers to the girls in the strip clubs.

All in all, God had healed me and healed other people through my testimony. How great is our God? I had overcome death more than once and I gave all the glory to God. Yes, I still have the brain tumor and migraines but I am healed, I believe it! It is done!

33

He's Better than a Doctor, He's Our Marvelous God

This book was supposed to have been completely written three months before I completed it, but some totally unexpected medical problems came up. Ann had just started her senior year of college, been there only two weeks, when I received a panicked call from her.

"Something is wrong with me, help me! I am very dizzy, the migraines are worse, I just want to sleep, my right arm is going numb, I am having full body tremors—but I am awake during them. I just don't feel well. Help me!"

I said I would call the doctor and call her right back. I called the doctor right away and she said Ann needed to be checked out immediately. Either she needed to get checked out locally, in Philadelphia, or I needed to bring her home to be looked at in Pittsburgh. When I called Ann and told her, she was worried about school and her studies. I told her that her health was more important than school. I told her I needed to get her home for an emergency MRI, CT scan and blood work. She insisted she did not want to go through it all again. I told her I understood, but we needed to figure out what was going on—we needed to go one step at a time. I insisted that she return home right away.

I called Pastor Shawn and his wife, Jen, and told them to pray. I prayed and called others to pray also. I got Ann home and right to the emergency room. They did an MRI and some blood work. The nurse asked Ann how she was feeling and she said, "Stop the pain in my head. And tell my mom and I what is going on." The nurse promised that as soon as they had the results, they would let us know. She asked if Ann wanted any pain medication for her migraines. Ann declined because nothing really worked. She just wanted to know why she was feeling so bad.

The MRI results came back and the doctor in the emergency room said there was no change. Her ventricles were the normal size and there was no change in the tumor. We would need to follow up with the neurologist. When I asked about the blood work, they said it was normal and that Ann would be fine. Ann and I just looked at each other. I was not pleased with what they told me. Ann was not acting right. I kept her home for a full week to monitor her. We were indeed thankful the tumor had not grown, but needed to know what was causing the other symptoms.

The neurosurgeon called a new neurologist and got Ann an emergency appointment. Dr. Rebecca met with us and said she had reviewed the MRI and everything looked fine. I told her that was what every neurologist says, but Ann was still having problems. *Why can't any doctor help her?* I thought. She then said something very interesting that no other neurologist had said to me before.

"Ann has a brain tumor. That is more like a trauma to the head than an illness. Many neurologists treat them like an illness and not the trauma they really are." She paused and said, "But something is puzzling me...her blood work."

"The emergency room doctors said her blood work showed everything was fine."

"Well, it's not. I want to do an extensive blood workup on Ann."

"That's fine...but what are you looking for?"

"I just want to make sure there weren't any lab errors. For her to have dizziness, numbness, and tremors, something has to be going on. I think the only way we can really tell is through an extensive blood workup. Ann, your examination is fine. You can go back to school, just keep in touch with me if you get any more symptoms. Also, before we leave, I want to say something, Dr. Rebecca, I feel it is time to kill this tumor."

"The only way I know to do that is through herbs. I have found herbs that will kill this tumor, if you are okay with Ann using them," I said.

"Absolutely," said Dr. Rebecca, "many of my patients would rather use herbs. I am okay with it. Ann, how about you?"

"Yes," she said. "I am also ready to kill this tumor."

"Ann will go back to school and we'll get the blood workup done and start the herbs," said Dr. Rebecca.

"Okay, I will expect your call about Ann's blood work results in a couple weeks," I said.

"Yes, they will be back then."

We left, finally at peace with a neurologist who understood and listened to Ann instead of saying, "I don't know."

Elizabeth and I drove Ann back to school. She started taking the new herbs and got the blood work done. I let Pastor Shawn and Jen know everything, and we all just kept praying that everything would turn out normal.

Fourteen days into taking the herbs, Ann's full body tremors stopped and limited only to her legs and arms—amazing. I had prayed about Ann starting on these new herbs and God had told me He would heal her through them when we used them again. I knew in my heart that I was doing the right thing. If God healed her organs completely through the herbs, He would heal whatever else was wrong. For our doctor to be in agreement with the herbs was great.

A month later, Dr. Rebecca called me to discuss Ann's blood work. She told me Ann's D2 was totally depleted. She explained that Vitamin D is very important for strong bones, general good health, and to help the immune system fight infections. That explained a lot about why she wasn't feeling well. Then I told her that Ann's tremors had decreased. She was happy to hear this, especially at only fourteen days into using the herbs. She said she would get Ann a prescription for high dose vitamin D and get it to her immediately. I asked if taking the herbs would be a problem with the vitamin D, since it was such a high dose. She said it would be fine. I called Ann and told her I would FedEx the vitamin D to her. We were both fine with all of this. I told Ann we were still waiting for the rest of the blood work results to come back and that I would let her know when they did. All this was happening as Ann was approaching the end of her final semester of college, when she would receive her credentials to become a youth pastor.

I was at work when I received a devastating phone call from Dr. Rebecca.

"The rest of the blood work has come back and Ann's ANA is a high positive. Ann has lupus. I made an emergency appointment for Ann at the end of November with the lupus doctor. We will go from there."

"When did all this happen? How? What are you talking about? I don't believe you... and I am not going to accept this. There is no way Ann has this," I said.

"I'm sorry," she said, "but Ann has lupus."

"Oh no, she doesn't have lupus."

"I know this is hard for you to accept, but you need to take care of the situation and not be in denial."

First thing, I called Jen. She didn't answer, so I hung up without leaving a message and called Pastor Shawn, crying. I was in total shock and didn't know what to do. He was also in shock, just like me. He couldn't believe it. He asked me the same questions I had asked Dr. Rebecca. I said I still had no answers. We prayed and asked God for guidance and peace. He asked me how and when was I going to tell Ann. I said I had no idea. I knew I had to tell her, but how do you call someone and give them this kind of news? We prayed again and asked God to give us wisdom on the best way to tell Ann.

I left work early that day, thinking all the way home about how I was going to tell Ann. I decided to call the dean and ask for his help. I explained what the doctor had told me and that I had promised Ann I would always be honest with her when the doctors told me anything. He arranged a conference call that included four of us: Ann, me, the dean, and the on campus pastor, Pastor Lily. I wanted her surrounded by people when I told her, given the distance between us (me at home, her at college). Ann was devastated when she heard the news. I explained that we would fight this together. I reminded her that this was an attack of Satan because he knows you are doing what God wants and he is trying to stop you.

That weekend, Ann came home and Pastor Billy Burke was in town. Something inside of me kept telling me go to the healing service with Ann. I knew it was the Holy Spirit, and I became very adamant on going. Ann was home because she had to see the lupus doctor on Tuesday. I KNEW that if I took her to the healing service, God WOULD HEAL HER! I truly believed we were going to get our miracle. That morning, Ann kept getting attacked by the enemy, telling her that lupus was killing her and eating up her organs. I told Ann, "I don't care what the devil said, we are going to see Pastor Billy and see a miracle from God in her, and that's final." Before the healing service, the Holy Spirit reminded me of the healing of the paralytic, the one whose four friends lowered him down through a roof before Jesus. I just knew in my heart that if I brought Ann to the healing service, she would be healed of lupus. All she needed was one touch from Jesus.

I remember saying to God, "We came to get Ann healed and we are not leaving until she gets the miracle. God, Ann has been through so much. We are not leaving until she gets her miracle. You said if we believed and asked in the name of Jesus, we would have our miracle. We want it now."

About a half hour later, Pastor Billy said God was healing lupus right now, that someone there had it, and they should go to him now for prayer. Needless to say, I walked Ann up to the front. When Pastor Billy prayed for Ann, I saw a peace come over her face, relief. Ann said to him, "I know in my heart that God healed me, but it was your prayer and God's touch, through you to me, that healed me of lupus. When we got back to our seats, we heard God say, "Ann is healed of lupus." We claimed it in the name of Jesus.

Ann's Account

When I first heard about the lupus, I got the news from a call from my mom. Pastor Lily called me into her office and the dean was there also. I was scared that I had done something wrong, because you just don't get called into Pastor Lily's office for a cup of coffee. Also, the dean was there and I was scared I was in major trouble. When my mom told me the doctor said that I had lupus, I broke down in tears. I couldn't believe that after the brain tumor drama, I now had another drama in my life—lupus. Pastor Lily and the dean prayed with my mom and I, and then I went home.

That Sunday, I was healed of lupus. It was not a ride in the park. I was being attacked by the enemy so much, I forgot about God's healing power. Whenever my mom tried to comfort me, in my mind, I was thinking, *Yeah, God, I am credentialed and this is happening?* When we went to Pastor Billy's healing service, I honestly did not want to go. I wanted to stay home and just not have to deal with it. Little did I know, God was going to heal me in the midst of my doubt. I know that God is the Healer, but I was believing the enemy's lies. Thankfully for my mom, she still took me. She knew beyond a shadow of a doubt that I was going to be healed that night of lupus, and I WAS! That night, I was healed of lupus and any other blood disease the enemy tried to place on me!

On Tuesday, my mom and I had to go to the lupus doctor. As we filled out the questionnaire for the doctor, we just put question marks on the form because I had none of the symptoms the paper said I should have. The doctor asked mom and I why we hadn't filled out the questionnaire. My mom said she couldn't because I didn't have any of the symptoms.

"Ann, how are you feeling," the doctor asked.

"Fine. I don't have what the papers say I should have."

"Well, your blood test showed positive for lupus. I don't understand. Do you mind if I just check you over to see if you don't have any symptoms?"

"Go ahead," I said.

"Do you have any rashes? Trouble walking? Swelling in the joints? Any difficulties?"

"No. The only reason we are here is because my blood test level came back high positive. I don't have any symptoms. I don't have lupus, just as my mom told you."

Still baffled, the doctor said, "Okay, I can't find anything wrong with you. You do not have lupus. But can we just do one more thing?"

My mom and I looked at each other, and she said, "What, exactly?"

"Can we just get blood work done, just to make sure?"

"You just said I don't have lupus," I said.

"I know I said that, but I just want to do another set of blood work to confirm what I said," replied the doctor.

"Just do it, Ann," my mom said. "We all are in agreement that you don't have it. Just do it to make her happy."

I knew the test would also confirm I did not have lupus. It would proclaim God's healing.

As I was getting my blood drawn, my mom heard God say, "Ann's blood is perfectly normal." My mom claimed it in Jesus' name.

Sometime later, my mom received the blood test results back and spoke with the doctor. Her words to my mom were, "I have never seen as perfect blood work as Ann's. Her blood levels are perfectly normal. I was still questioning lupus in the back of my mind, even though I told you in the office that she had no symptoms. But now with the blood work, I see she definitely does not have lupus. This is the confirmation."

"No, the confirmation came from God," my mom said. "Ann is healed of lupus. We told you she doesn't have it."

God I am so thankful that You have shown yourself mightily in my life, even despite my doubt. I know that I still have the brain tumor, migraines, hydrocephalus, and tremors. I know that you are not finished with the rest of the healing miracle. I am still expecting to receive the rest of my miracle in Jesus' name. All the glory to God. Nothing is impossible with You, God. Amen and Amen!

Cindy's Words

Ann graduated from college and earned her Youth Pastor credentials with the Assemblies of God. We are excited to see the rest of the outcome in Ann's life. My advice to you is, don't stop believing, for we serve a wonderful, faithful God who is always true to His Word, "so is my word that goes from my mouth: it will not return to me empty, but will accomplish what I desire and achieve the purpose for which I sent it" (Isaiah 55:11, NIV).

www.ingramcontent.com/pod-product-compliance
Lightning Source LLC
Chambersburg PA
CBHW030328080526
44584CB00012B/766